Better Homes and Gardens®

Home-Style Cooking

On the cover: When it comes to flavor, it's hard to beat a good pot roast mingled with a variety of vegetables and simmered to tender perfection. So, why not treat your family to *Beef and Bean Pot Roast*, a great-tasting variation of an old standby.

Above: This festive yeast bread assortment includes frosting-drizzled *Cinnamon Whirl*, *Bubble Wreath* (flavored with cinnamon-sugar and nuts), fruit-filled *Swedish Tea Wreath*, and cardamom-spiced *Sugar Plum Loaf*. (See Index for page numbers.)

Contents

BETTER HOMES AND GARDENS BOOKS
Editorial Director: Don Dooley
Managing Editor: Malcolm E. Robinson   Art Director: John Berg
Asst. Managing Editor: Lawrence D. Clayton   Asst. Art Director: Randall Yontz
Food Editor: Nancy Morton
Senior Food Editor: Joyce Trollope
Associate Editors: Sandra Granseth, Sharyl Heiken, Rosemary C. Hutchinson, Elizabeth Strait
Assistant Editor: Diane Jesse
Designers: Candy Carleton, Harijs Priekulis, Faith Berven
Contributing Editor: Lorene Frohling

Our seal assures you that every recipe in *Home-Style Cooking* is endorsed by the Better Homes and Gardens Test Kitchen. Each recipe is thoroughly tested for family appeal, practicality, and deliciousness.

What is home-style cooking?

Home-style cooking is food at its best. It's a relaxed way
of cooking that turns everyday ingredients into
downright good food. It kindles happy thoughts of tantalizing
aromas that were so much a part of Grandma's kitchen
long ago. And, it bears a marked resemblance to the foods
you found irresistible during childhood.

Home-style cooking takes on a regional flavor in many
areas of the United States. The first section of
the book pays tribute to regional cooking, which often makes
use of locally abundant ingredients. As with all
regional dishes, slight variations exist from one family to
the next. Nevertheless, many of the foods have gained
fame and attention in locales far removed from their origin.

The next section is a family album of old-fashioned
recipes brought up to date. Because of their appeal and
practicality, many of these recipes have survived
several generations of family enjoyment with little change
other than the refinement of measurements and cooking
methods. Others have become classics in their own right
without the use of expensive ingredients or lavish sauces.

The third section offers menu suggestions for
home-cooked meals planned around activity-oriented events,
special family occasions, and community socials.
Some are planned for eating at home, while others travel to
the activity site with little fuss and bother.

The final section is a treasury of recipes for preserving
fresh fruits and vegetables from the garden. Just
as in Grandma's day, home-canned pickles, relishes, jellies,
and jams are still a source of pride and accomplishment
as well as an economical means of feeding the family.

◀ **The old-fashioned goodness** of home cooking is as fashionable today as
it was yesterday. Homemade favorites shown here include *Sausage
Supper, Date-Filled Sugar Cookies, Deep-Dish Apple Pie, Double-Decker
Potatoes,* and *Corn-Stuffed Pork Chops.* (See Index for page numbers.)

Cross-Country Family Cooking

In many areas of our country, home cooking is a regional art passed from one generation to the next. This chapter focuses on some of America's distinctive regional foods.

In the South, cooking reflects the genteel life-style of a proud people. Up North, New Englanders and the Pennsylvania Dutch continue the sensible and practical approach to cooking practiced by their forefathers. Farther west and inland, Midwestern and Northwestern cooking mirrors the bounty of the land as well as the ethnic backgrounds of the early settlers.

Western cooking, the youngest of all, reflects an easygoing people in a mild climate. Outdoor cooking and foreign influences are part of this imaginative style.

Popular dishes from each of the regions include: Mid- and Northwest—*Salmon with Wild Rice* and *Apple Cider Pie;* East and Northeast—*Baked Beans* and *Brown Bread;* South—*Ambrosia* and *Creole Gumbo;* and West—*Mustard Barbecued Ribs, Sopaipillas,* and *Western Tossed Salad.* (See Index for page numbers.)

Down-South Cooking

Southern cooking ranges from the Creole foods of New Orleans to other Southern favorites including ham, pork, chicken, and seafood. Good cooks of the South have a knack for flavoring their foods with salt pork or bacon.

Mainstays in the diet include grits, greens, and black-eyed peas. Hot breads also appear in many a southern meal, whether it be corn bread, hush puppies, or piping-hot biscuits.

Angel Pie

    3 egg whites
    1 teaspoon vanilla
    1 cup sugar
    1 cup finely crushed graham
        crackers (14 crackers)
    1 cup chopped pecans
    1 teaspoon baking powder
    ½ cup whipping cream

Beat egg whites and vanilla to soft peaks; gradually add sugar, beating till stiff peaks form. Mix crumbs, nuts, and baking powder; fold into beaten whites. Spread evenly in greased and floured 9-inch pie plate. Bake at 325° for 20 to 25 minutes. Cool completely. Whip the cream. Cut pie; top with cream. Serves 6.

Poppy Seed Dressing

    ¾ cup sugar
    ⅓ cup vinegar
    1 teaspoon dry mustard
    1 teaspoon grated onion
    1 cup salad oil
    1 tablespoon poppy seed
        Grapefruit sections
        Avocado slices
        Lettuce

Combine first 4 ingredients and 1 teaspoon salt. Add oil slowly, beating with electric mixer or rotary beater till thick. Stir in poppy seed. Cover; chill. Stir well before serving. Serve over grapefruit and avocado arranged on lettuce-lined plates. Makes 1¾ cups dressing.

Deviled Crab

    1 pound fresh or frozen crab meat
    1 cup mayonnaise or salad
        dressing
    2 slightly beaten eggs
    1 tablespoon Worcestershire sauce
    2 teaspoons grated onion
        Dash bottled hot pepper sauce
    2 cups soft bread crumbs
        (2½ slices bread)
    2 tablespoons butter or
        margarine, melted

Thaw crab, if frozen; remove any bits of shell. Leave crab in chunks. Mix mayonnaise and next 4 ingredients; stir in crab. Spoon into 6 to 8 crab shells, coquilles, or individual baking dishes. Toss crumbs with butter; sprinkle atop crab. Bake at 350° till bubbly and brown, 15 to 20 minutes. Serve with lemon wedges, if desired. Makes 6 to 8 servings.

Baked Carrots and Apples

    8 medium carrots, cut in ½-inch
        pieces (4 cups)
    6 apples, peeled, cored, and
        sliced (3 cups)
    ¼ cup honey
    2 tablespoons butter or margarine
        Paprika

Cook carrots, covered, in boiling salted water till tender, 12 to 15 minutes; drain. Stir in apples and honey. Turn into 9-inch pie plate; dot with butter. Cover; bake at 350° for 50 to 55 minutes. Stir; sprinkle with paprika. Bake, uncovered, 10 minutes. Serves 8.

Southern cooks depend on locally abundant ingredients for many of their specialties. Recipes shown here are *Deviled Crab* heaped into crab shells, *Poppy Seed Dressing* drizzled over grapefruit and avocado slices, *Baked Carrots and Apples* sweetened with honey, and *Angel Pie* rich with pecans.

Georgia-Style Brunswick Stew

A robust stew thickened with torn bread—

1 pound beef chuck
1 pound pork shoulder
½ pound lamb shoulder
3 cups diced, peeled, raw
   potatoes (3 medium)
2 cups chopped peeled tomatoes
   or 1 16-ounce can tomatoes,
   cut up
2 cups fresh lima beans *or* 1 10-
   ounce package frozen lima
   beans
1 cup chopped onion
2 cups fresh corn cut from cob *or*
   1 10-ounce package frozen
   whole kernel corn
1 tablespoon sugar
2 teaspoons salt
½ teaspoon dried basil, crushed
¼ teaspoon dried thyme, crushed
¼ teaspoon pepper
1 bay leaf, crushed
2 slices white bread

Cut all meats in ½-inch cubes; place in 6-quart kettle with water to cover. Bring to boiling; reduce heat. Simmer, covered, till tender, about 1 hour. Remove meat. Measure broth; if necessary, add water to measure 4 cups. Return broth to kettle; bring to boiling.

Add potatoes, undrained tomatoes, beans, and onion. Cook, covered, till tender, about 12 minutes. Add meat, corn, and next 6 ingredients; cook, covered, 3 minutes. Season to taste with additional salt and pepper. Break bread into pieces; add to stew, stirring constantly. Chill overnight to blend flavors. Reheat before serving. Makes 8 to 10 servings.

Hush Puppies

Stir together 1½ cups white cornmeal, ¼ cup all-purpose flour, 1 tablespoon baking powder, and ¾ teaspoon salt. Add ¾ cup buttermilk, 2 beaten eggs, and ¼ cup finely chopped onion; beat well. Drop batter by level tablespoonfuls into ½ inch hot lard *or* cooking oil. Cook till golden brown, about 3 minutes; turn once. Drain on paper toweling; place in warm oven while frying remaining batter. Makes 24.

Creole Gumbo

This southern specialty is shown on page 6—

1 4-pound stewing chicken
3 cups cubed fully cooked ham
1½ cups chopped onion
1 cup chopped okra
1 8-ounce can tomato sauce
⅛ teaspoon cayenne
   Few drops bottled hot pepper
   sauce
1 pint shucked oysters
2 cups chopped peeled tomatoes
2 tablespoons filé powder
   Hot cooked rice

Place chicken in Dutch oven. Add 6 cups water and 2 teaspoons salt. Bring to boiling. Reduce heat; simmer till tender, about 2 hours. Cool. Remove meat and cube. Skim fat from broth. Strain broth; return to Dutch oven. Add chicken, ham, onion, okra, tomato sauce, cayenne, and hot pepper sauce. Drain oysters, adding liquid to Dutch oven. Bring to boiling. Reduce heat; simmer 1 hour. Add oysters and tomato; simmer 10 minutes. Beat a moderate amount of broth into filé; stir into gumbo. Do not cook further. Serve over rice. Serves 12.

Ham Hocks and Greens

1 pound mustard greens
8 ounces turnip greens
8 ounces collard greens
3½ pounds ham hocks
   Corn Bread

Wash greens; drain. In large kettle brown the ham hocks. Add 4 cups water; bring to boiling. Add greens; return to boiling. Reduce heat; simmer, covered, 1½ hours. Prepare Corn Bread. To serve, ladle greens and juices (pot liquor) into bowl; garnish with hard-cooked egg slices, if desired. Serve ham hocks in another bowl; spoon juices over Corn Bread squares. Serves 4.

Corn Bread: Stir 1 cup all-purpose flour with 1 cup yellow cornmeal, ¼ cup sugar, 4 teaspoons baking powder, and ¾ teaspoon salt. Add 1 cup milk, 2 eggs, and ¼ cup cooking oil. Beat with rotary beater or electric mixer just till smooth, about 1 minute; do not overbeat. Bake in greased 9x9x2-inch baking pan at 350° for 20 to 25 minutes. Cut into squares.

Beef Bamboula

½ pound ground pork
1 cup finely chopped celery
¼ cup chopped onion
1 teaspoon instant beef
    bouillon granules
1 cup milk
¼ cup all-purpose flour
2 tablespoons snipped parsley
2 tablespoons sliced pitted
    ripe olives
1 tablespoon catsup
    Pastry for 2-crust 9-inch pie
1½ cups chopped cooked beef

Brown the pork; drain. Set aside. In saucepan combine celery, onion, bouillon granules, and ¾ cup water. Cover; simmer 10 minutes. Do not drain. Blend milk into flour; stir into celery mixture. Cook and stir till slightly thickened and bubbly. Stir in pork, parsley, olives, catsup, ¾ teaspoon salt, and ¼ teaspoon pepper. Bring to boiling; set aside.

Line 9-inch pie plate with pastry. Spoon beef on bottom crust; top with pork mixture. Adjust top crust; seal. Cut slits for escape of steam. Fold foil strip around rim to avoid overbrowning. Bake at 400° till golden brown, 30 to 35 minutes. Let stand 15 minutes before serving. Makes 6 servings.

Hot Bean and Pork Salad

12 ounces fresh green beans
6 cups torn romaine
1 small onion, thinly sliced
    and separated into rings
    Freshly ground black pepper
4 ounces salt pork
¼ cup tarragon vinegar
2 tablespoons chopped
    canned pimiento

Wash beans and remove ends; cut into 1-inch pieces. Cook in small amount of boiling salted water till crisp-tender, about 10 minutes; drain. Combine romaine and onion; sprinkle with pepper. Finely chop salt pork; cook in skillet till crisp and browned; remove from heat. Stir in vinegar, pimiento, and 2 tablespoons water; add beans. Heat. Pour over romaine mixture; toss. Serve at once. Serves 6.

Jambalaya

12 ounces fresh or frozen
    shelled shrimp
4 slices bacon
½ cup chopped onion
½ cup chopped celery
1 clove garlic, minced
1 28-ounce can tomatoes, cut up
2 cups water
1 cup uncooked regular rice
3 tablespoons canned tomato paste
2 teaspoons instant chicken
    bouillon granules
1 teaspoon sugar
½ teaspoon dried thyme, crushed
¼ teaspoon cayenne
    Few drops bottled hot pepper
    sauce
2 cups cubed fully cooked ham
1 large green pepper, cut in
    strips
    Snipped parsley

Thaw shrimp, if frozen. In Dutch oven cook bacon till crisp; remove and crumble, reserving drippings. In reserved drippings cook onion, celery, and garlic till tender. Stir in undrained tomatoes, water, rice, tomato paste, bouillon granules, sugar, thyme, cayenne, and hot pepper sauce. Bring to boiling; stir occasionally. Reduce heat; simmer, covered, till rice is tender, about 20 minutes. Add shrimp, ham, and green pepper; simmer, uncovered, till of desired consistency and shrimp are pink, 5 to 10 minutes. Turn into serving bowl; top with bacon and parsley. Pass additional hot pepper sauce, if desired. Serves 8.

Spicy Crawfish Boil

Thoroughly rinse 6 pounds live crawfish in fresh water. In large kettle combine 3 gallons water; 4 stalks celery, quartered; 2 onions, quartered; 2 lemons, quartered; ½ cup salt; 4 bay leaves; 4 cloves garlic, minced; 2 tablespoons crushed dried red pepper; 1 teaspoon dried thyme, crushed; ½ teaspoon cayenne; and 8 whole cloves. Bring to boiling; add crawfish. Return to boiling; cook till crawfish turn deep red, about 5 minutes. Drain. Serve crawfish with melted butter. Serves 4.

Black Bean Soup

2 cups dry black beans
  (16 ounces)
¼ cup chopped onion
¼ cup butter *or* margarine
2 stalks celery, cut up
2½ teaspoons salt
  Dash pepper
¼ cup dry sherry (optional)
2 hard-cooked eggs, chopped
1 lemon, thinly sliced

Cover beans with water; soak overnight. Drain; rinse thoroughly. In large kettle or Dutch oven cook onion in butter till tender but not brown. Add beans, celery, and 10 cups water. Cover; simmer till beans are soft, 3 to 3½ hours. Remove from heat. Place part of the bean mixture at a time in blender container; cover and blend till smooth. (Or, rub beans with liquid through sieve.) Return mixture to saucepan. Stir in salt and pepper; heat soup just to boiling. Stir in sherry just before serving, if desired. Garnish servings with chopped eggs and lemon slices. Makes 8 servings.

Hopping John

1¼ cups dry black-eyed peas
  (8 ounces)
1½ cups sliced onion
1 large clove garlic, minced
1 bay leaf
½ teaspoon pepper
¼ teaspoon crushed dried
  red pepper
8 ounces salt pork, rinsed and
  cut in 12 pieces
3 cups hot cooked rice

Rinse peas. In 3-quart covered saucepan bring peas and 4 cups water to boiling. Boil 2 minutes; remove from heat. Let stand 1 hour. (Or, add peas to 4 cups water; soak overnight.) Do not drain. Add onion, garlic, bay leaf, pepper, and red pepper. Bring to boiling; simmer, covered, 1 hour. Stir occasionally. Stir in salt pork; simmer, uncovered, till peas are tender, 50 to 60 minutes. Stir often. Remove salt pork and bay leaf; mash peas slightly. Season to taste with additional salt, if desired. Serve with rice. Makes 4 to 6 servings.

Okra and Tomatoes

¼ cup sliced scallions *or*
  green onions
2 tablespoons butter *or* margarine
1 tablespoon all-purpose flour
½ teaspoon salt
½ cup milk
¼ cup shredded sharp American
  cheese (1 ounce)
8 ounces fresh okra pods, cut in
  ½-inch slices and cooked, *or* 1
  10-ounce package frozen cut
  okra, cooked and drained
2 medium tomatoes, peeled and
  chopped (1¾ cups)
¾ cup soft bread crumbs
  (1 slice bread)
1 tablespoon butter *or*
  margarine, melted

Cook scallions in 2 tablespoons butter till tender but not brown. Blend in flour and salt. Add milk all at once; cook and stir till thickened and bubbly. Stir in cheese till melted. Fold in okra and tomato. Turn into 1-quart casserole. Toss crumbs with melted butter; sprinkle around edge of casserole. Bake at 350° till hot, about 30 minutes. Serves 6.

Ambrosia

This fruit combo is shown on page 7 —

1 13¼-ounce can pineapple chunks
3 medium oranges, sectioned
½ cup maraschino cherries,
  drained and halved
½ cup shredded coconut

Drain pineapple, reserving ¼ cup of the syrup. Combine pineapple, oranges, cherries, and reserved syrup. Cover; chill. Just before serving, fold in coconut. Garnish with fresh mint leaves, if desired. Makes 6 servings.

The South is well known for its use of vegetables and corn bread. Among those dishes savored by all who either visit or live below the Mason-Dixon Line are cheesy *Okra and Tomatoes*, peppery hot *Hopping John*, smooth and hearty *Black Bean Soup*, and classic *Corn Bread* (see recipe, page 10).

East and Northeast Family Favorites

Lobsters, clams, scallops, and cod rate high in New England. Likewise, this area is known for its baked beans, brown bread, clam chowder, maple syrup, cranberries, and corned beef. Further down the coast, the large cities offer a variety of ethnic cooking and imported foods. Inland, the thrifty Pennsylvania Dutch prepare good food from simple ingredients.

Steamed Clams

Cover soft-shelled clams in shells with salt water (⅓ cup salt to 1 gallon cold water). Let stand 15 minutes; rinse. Repeat twice more. Place clams on rack in kettle with 1 cup hot water. Cover pan tightly; steam just till shells open, about 5 minutes. Discard clams that do not open. Serve in shells with melted butter. Allow 15 to 20 clams per person.

Cod Cakes

      8 ounces salt cod
      3 cups diced, peeled, raw
            potatoes (3 medium)
      1 beaten egg
      2 tablespoons butter *or* margarine
      ¾ cup finely crushed saltine
            crackers (about 21 crackers)
      Fat for frying

Soak cod in enough water to cover for 12 hours. Drain; dice fish (about 1⅔ cups). Cook potatoes and cod, covered, in boiling unsalted water till potatoes are tender, about 15 minutes; drain. Beat with electric mixer. Add egg, butter, and ⅛ teaspoon pepper; beat well. Using about ¼ cup mixture for each, shape into 2½- to 3-inch cakes, ½ inch thick. Coat with cracker crumbs. Fry in deep hot fat (375°) for 2 minutes; turn. Fry till golden, about 2 minutes more. Trim with lemon and parsley, if desired. Makes about 12 cakes.

Turkey with Oyster Stuffing

      1 10- to 12-pound turkey
      1 cup chopped onion
      6 tablespoons butter *or* margarine
      1 pint shucked oysters
      6 cups dry bread cubes
      ¼ cup snipped parsley
      1 teaspoon dried thyme, crushed
            Cooking oil

Remove giblets from turkey; cover giblets with water. Simmer till tender, 1½ to 2 hours. Drain; reserve liquid. Dice giblets; set aside. Cook onion in butter till tender; set aside. Drain oysters; reserve liquid. Chop oysters. Combine oysters, giblets, onion, bread, parsley, thyme, ½ teaspoon salt, and ¼ teaspoon pepper. Toss with oyster liquid and enough giblet liquid to moisten. Salt cavities of bird; stuff. Tuck legs under band of skin or tie to tail. Place on rack in shallow roasting pan; rub skin with oil. Cap with foil. Roast at 325° till thermometer registers 185°, 4½ to 5 hours.

Mulled Cranberry Cider

Combine one 48-ounce bottle cranberry juice cocktail (6 cups), one 32-ounce bottle apple cider (4 cups), ½ cup packed brown sugar, 3 inches stick cinnamon, 1 teaspoon whole allspice, and 1 teaspoon whole cloves. Bring to boiling. Reduce heat; simmer, covered, 20 minutes. Remove spices. Serve with lemon slices and cinnamon stick stirrers. Makes 10 cups.

New Englanders relish many of the same foods that ▶ their forefathers labored to provide for their families in early colonial times. Traditional dishes shown here are *Steamed Clams, Mulled Cranberry Cider, Turkey with Oyster Stuffing, Cod Cakes,*and *New England Boiled Dinner* (see recipe, page 16).

New England Boiled Dinner

Often served on Sunday in early colonial homes, this meal-on-a-platter is shown on page 15 —

    1 3- to 4-pound corned beef
       brisket
    4 ounces salt pork (optional)
      • • •
    6 small onions
    4 medium potatoes, peeled and
       quartered
    4 medium carrots, quartered
    3 medium parsnips, peeled
       and cut in chunks
    2 medium rutabagas, peeled
       and cubed
    1 small cabbage, cored
       and cut in wedges

Place corned beef in large kettle or Dutch oven; add water to cover. Add salt pork, if desired. Bring to boiling; reduce heat and simmer, covered, till tender, about 2½ hours.

Remove meat and salt pork. Add all vegetables *except cabbage* to cooking liquid. Cover; cook 15 minutes. Add cabbage; cover and cook till cabbage is tender, 15 to 20 minutes. Return meat to kettle; heat through. Remove meat and vegetables to serving platter. Season to taste with salt and pepper. Makes 6 to 8 servings.

Red Flannel Hash

A Yankee favorite using leftover corned beef —

    ⅓ cup finely chopped onion
    2 tablespoons shortening
    3 cups finely chopped cooked
       potatoes
    1 16-ounce can beets, drained and
       finely chopped
  1½ cups finely chopped cooked
       corned beef
    ⅓ cup milk
    ½ teaspoon salt
    1 or 2 drops bottled hot
       pepper sauce

In skillet cook onion in hot shortening till tender. Lightly toss together potatoes, beets, corned beef, milk, salt, and hot pepper sauce. Spread hash mixture evenly in skillet. Cook over medium heat till bottom is browned; turn occasionally with spatula. Serves 4.

Baked Beans

This hearty bean recipe is shown on page 7 —

    2 cups dry navy beans (1 pound)
    ½ cup molasses
    ⅓ cup packed brown sugar
    1 teaspoon dry mustard
    ⅛ teaspoon pepper
    4 ounces salt pork, quartered
    1 medium onion, chopped (½ cup)

Rinse beans. In large, heavy saucepan combine beans and 8 cups water; soak overnight. (Or, bring beans and 8 cups water to boiling; boil 2 minutes. Remove from heat. Cover; let stand 1 hour.) Do not drain. Add ½ teaspoon salt to beans; bring to boiling. Reduce heat; simmer, covered, till tender, about 1 hour. Drain; reserve bean liquid.

Combine molasses, brown sugar, mustard, pepper, and ½ teaspoon salt; stir in *2 cups* of the reserved liquid. In 2-quart bean pot or casserole combine beans, salt pork, onion, and molasses mixture; stir till blended. Cover and bake at 300° for 3½ hours. Stir beans occasionally; stir in a little of the reserved bean liquid or water, if necessary, for moistness. Makes 6 to 8 servings.

Brown Bread

Accompany with beans, as pictured on page 7 —

    2 cups buttermilk
    ¾ cup dark molasses
    1 cup raisins
    1 cup whole wheat flour
    1 cup rye flour
    1 cup yellow cornmeal
    ¾ teaspoon baking soda
    ½ teaspoon salt

In mixing bowl blend buttermilk and molasses. Stir in raisins. Stir together whole wheat flour, rye flour, cornmeal, soda, and salt; stir into buttermilk mixture till blended.

Divide batter among 3 greased 20-ounce clean food cans. (Or, fill four 16-ounce cans.) Cover tightly with foil; place on rack set in large Dutch oven. Add boiling water to depth of 1 inch. Cover and simmer over low heat; steam till done, 2½ to 3 hours. Add more boiling water, as needed. Remove from cans; cool on rack. Makes 3 or 4 loaves.

New England Clam Chowder

      24 medium quahog clams *or* 2 7½-
         ounce cans minced clams *or*
       1 pint shucked clams
       4 ounces salt pork, minced
       4 cups diced, peeled,
         raw potatoes
       ½ cup chopped onion
      1¾ cups milk
       1 cup light cream
       ¼ cup milk
       3 tablespoons all-purpose flour
      1½ teaspoons salt

If using clams in shell, place in large kettle; add 1 cup water. Cover; bring to boiling. Reduce heat; steam just till shells open, 5 to 10 minutes. Discard clams that do not open. Remove clams from shells. Dice clams, reserving ½ cup clam liquor. In saucepan cook salt pork till crisp. Remove any lean pork; reserve. To drippings add potatoes, onion, reserved clam liquor, and 1½ cups water. Cook, covered, till potatoes are tender, 15 to 20 minutes. Add clams, 1¾ cups milk, and cream. Stir ¼ cup milk into flour; stir into soup. Heat to boiling; stir occasionally. Stir in salt, dash white pepper, and reserved pork. Serves 6.

Sally Lunn

       1 package active dry yeast
       ¼ cup warm water (110°)
       ½ cup sugar
       2 tablespoons lard
       2 eggs
       1 teaspoon salt
      3½ cups all-purpose flour
       1 cup warm milk (110°)

Soften yeast in warm water. In mixing bowl cream sugar and lard. Beat in eggs and salt. Stir in *1½ cups* of the flour; beat vigorously. Stir in milk and softened yeast; mix well. Add remaining flour; beat vigorously.

   Cover; let rise in warm place till double (about 1 hour). Stir down batter; spoon evenly into greased 10-inch fluted tube pan. Cover; let rise again till double (30 to 45 minutes). Bake at 325° for 10 minutes. Increase oven temperature to 375°; bake 20 minutes more. Remove from pan. Serve warm or cool.

Chicken-Corn Soup

      10 cups chicken broth
       1 2½-pound ready-to-cook broiler-
         fryer chicken, cut up
       2 celery stalks, cut in 3-inch
         pieces
       1 teaspoon salt
       1 teaspoon whole peppercorns
       ½ cup finely chopped celery
       ¼ cup snipped parsley
         Homemade Noodles
       2 12-ounce cans whole kernel corn
         Dash thread saffron

In large kettle or Dutch oven combine first 5 ingredients; bring to boiling. Reduce heat; simmer, covered, till chicken is done, about 45 minutes. Remove chicken; cool. Remove meat from bones; cube and set aside. Discard bones. Strain broth; return to kettle. Add chopped celery, parsley, and dash pepper. Bring to boiling; stir in Homemade Noodles, undrained corn, and saffron. Simmer till noodles are done, about 15 minutes. Stir in cubed chicken; heat through. Serves 8 to 10.

   Homemade Noodles: Combine 1 beaten egg, 2 tablespoons milk, and ½ teaspoon salt. Add enough all-purpose flour to make a stiff dough, about 1 cup. Roll very thin on floured surface; let stand 20 minutes. Roll up loosely; slice ¼ inch wide. Unroll dough. Spread noodles apart; let dry 2 hours. (If desired, store in covered container till needed.)

Maple-Nut Acorn Squash

       3 acorn squash
       3 tablespoons butter *or* margarine
       2 tablespoons maple-flavored
         syrup
       ¼ teaspoon salt
       ¼ teaspoon ground cinnamon
       ⅛ teaspoon ground allspice
       2 tablespoons chopped walnuts

Halve squash; remove seeds. Place, cut side down, in greased, shallow baking pan. Bake at 350° till tender, 50 to 60 minutes. Scoop out pulp, leaving a thin shell. Combine pulp, butter, syrup, salt, and spices; spoon into shells. Top with nuts. Bake at 350° till heated through, 10 to 15 minutes. Makes 6 servings.

Red Cabbage with Apples

A "sweet and sour" specialty from the Pennsylvania Dutch—

2 tablespoons bacon drippings
¼ cup packed brown sugar
¼ cup vinegar
¼ cup water
½ teaspoon salt
Dash pepper
1 small onion
4 or 5 whole cloves
4 cups shredded red cabbage
(½ medium head)
2 cups sliced peeled apples

In medium skillet heat bacon drippings; blend in brown sugar, vinegar, water, salt, and pepper. Stick onion with whole cloves. Add to skillet with shredded cabbage and apple slices. Cover and cook over low heat, stirring occasionally, 25 to 30 minutes. Discard onion. Spoon into serving bowl. Serves 6 to 8.

Cracker Pudding

2 cups milk
2 beaten egg yolks
¼ cup sugar
1 cup coarsely crushed saltine
crackers (22 crackers)
½ cup shredded coconut
1 teaspoon vanilla
2 egg whites
¼ cup sugar

In medium saucepan slowly stir milk into egg yolks. Add ¼ cup sugar. Cook and stir over medium heat till mixture is bubbly; remove from heat. Stir in cracker crumbs, coconut, and vanilla. Pour into 1-quart casserole.

Beat egg whites till soft peaks form; gradually add ¼ cup sugar, beating till stiff peaks form. Carefully spread beaten egg whites over hot pudding. Bake at 350° for 12 to 15 minutes. Serve immediately or cool to room temperature. Makes 6 to 8 servings.

Thrifty and simple, Pennsylvania Dutch cooking is good food prepared in an imaginative way. Some of the foods typical of the friendly people in the Lancaster area of Pennsylvania include *Beef Stew and Potato Dumplings, Red Cabbage with Apples,* and spicy-sweet *Chowchow* (see recipe, page 87).

Beef Stew and Potato Dumplings

    2 tablespoons all-purpose flour
    ½ teaspoon salt
    ⅛ teaspoon pepper
    1½ pounds beef stew meat
    2 onions, sliced
    2 tablespoons bacon drippings
    1 10½-ounce can condensed
        beef broth
    ¾ cup water
    1 tablespoon vinegar
    3 medium carrots, peeled and
        sliced ½ inch thick (1 cup)
    Potato Dumplings
    Snipped parsley

Combine flour, salt, and pepper; coat meat with flour mixture. In Dutch oven cook meat and onion in bacon drippings till onion is tender and meat is browned. Stir in broth, water, and vinegar; add carrots. Bring to boiling; reduce heat. Simmer, covered, till meat is tender, about 1½ hours. Drop Potato Dumplings on bubbling stew. Cover; simmer 15 minutes. Sprinkle with parsley. Makes 5 servings.

Potato Dumplings: Combine 1 beaten egg, ¾ cup soft bread crumbs (1 slice bread), 1 tablespoon all-purpose flour, 1 tablespoon finely chopped onion, 1 tablespoon snipped parsley, ½ teaspoon salt, and dash pepper; stir in 2½ cups finely shredded, peeled, raw potato (2 large). With floured fingers, form mixture into ten 2-inch balls. Lightly dust with all-purpose flour before dropping onto stew.

Shoofly Pie

    1½ cups all-purpose flour
    ½ cup sugar
    ¼ teaspoon baking soda
    ¼ cup butter *or* margarine
    ½ cup light molasses
    ½ cup hot water
    ¼ teaspoon baking soda
    1 unbaked 8-inch pastry shell

Stir together first 3 ingredients; cut in butter till crumbly. Mix molasses, water, and ¼ teaspoon soda. Pour ⅓ of the molasses mixture into unbaked shell; sprinkle with ⅓ of the flour mixture. Repeat layers, ending with flour. Bake at 375° about 40 minutes. Cool.

Apple Pandowdy

The dessert is "dowdied" when the crust is broken up and stirred into the apple mixture—

    Pastry for 2-crust 9-inch pie
    ¼ cup butter *or* margarine, melted
    ½ cup sugar
    ½ teaspoon ground cinnamon
    ¼ teaspoon ground nutmeg
    10 cups thinly sliced peeled
        apples (10 large apples)
    ½ cup light molasses
    ¼ cup water
    3 tablespoons butter *or*
        margarine, melted

Roll pastry to 15x11-inch rectangle; brush with *some* of the ¼ cup melted butter. Fold in half. Brush and fold again; seal edges. Repeat rolling, brushing, and folding. Chill.

Mix sugar, spices, and dash salt; toss with apples. Place in 13x9x2-inch baking dish. Mix molasses and remaining ingredients; pour over apples. Roll pastry to 15x11-inch rectangle. Place over apples; turn edges under and flute. Bake at 400° for 10 minutes. Reduce heat to 325°; bake 30 minutes. Remove from oven. "Dowdy" the crust by cutting through crust and apples with sharp knife. Bake 10 minutes more. Serve warm. Serves 6 to 8.

Strawberry Flummery

    ⅓ cup sugar
    ¼ cup cornstarch
    ¼ teaspoon salt
    3 cups milk
    1 beaten egg yolk
    2 teaspoons vanilla
    2 cups fresh strawberries, halved
    2 tablespoons sugar

In saucepan combine first 3 ingredients; blend in milk. Cook and stir over medium heat till thickened and bubbly. Stir a moderate amount of hot mixture into egg yolk; return all to saucepan. Cook and stir over low heat till thickened, 1 to 2 minutes. Remove from heat; stir in vanilla. Pour into 1½-quart serving bowl; cover surface with plastic wrap or waxed paper. Cool; chill for 2 hours.

Sprinkle berries with 2 tablespoons sugar. Arrange atop pudding; serve at once. Serves 6.

Cooking in the Mid- and Northwest

The diverse cooking of the Midwest reflects its immigrant heritage as well as the wide variety of foods raised in this area. Corn, wheat, and dairy products are plenteous in the region and appear in many midwestern menus along with beef, pork, and freshwater fish.

Specialties of the Northwest region include seafood, fresh fruits, and wild berries.

Lentil Soup

2 cups dry lentils
2 slices bacon, diced
½ cup chopped onion
½ cup chopped celery
¼ cup chopped carrot
3 tablespoons snipped parsley
1 clove garlic, minced
2½ teaspoons salt
½ teaspoon dried oregano, crushed
¼ teaspoon pepper
1 16-ounce can tomatoes, cut up
2 tablespoons wine vinegar

Rinse lentils; drain. Place in large kettle with 8 cups water. Add remaining ingredients except tomatoes and vinegar. Cover; simmer 1½ hours. Add undrained tomatoes and vinegar. Simmer, covered, 30 minutes longer. Season to taste with salt and pepper. Serves 8 to 10.

Pork-Applesauce-Kraut Bake

Trim excess fat from 4 pork shoulder chops, cut ½ inch thick (2 pounds). In skillet cook trimmings till 1 tablespoon fat accumulates; discard trimmings. Brown the chops slowly on both sides in hot fat. Remove chops; drain off excess fat. Combine one 16-ounce can sauerkraut, undrained and snipped (2 cups); one 8½-ounce can applesauce (1 cup); ¼ cup finely chopped onion; 2 tablespoons packed brown sugar; and ¾ teaspoon caraway seed. Pour into skillet; top with chops. Season with salt and pepper. Cover; simmer till chops are tender, 35 to 45 minutes. Makes 4 servings.

Chopped Beef Pasties

3 cups all-purpose flour
1½ teaspoons salt
1 cup shortening
7 to 8 tablespoons cold water
• • •
1 pound beef round steak, cut in ¼-inch cubes
2 or 3 medium potatoes, peeled and coarsely chopped (2 cups)
1 medium turnip, peeled and cut in ¼-inch cubes (¾ cup)
½ cup finely chopped onion
1½ teaspoons salt
¼ teaspoon pepper
½ cup catsup
¼ cup water

In mixing bowl combine flour and 1½ teaspoons salt; cut in shortening till mixture resembles coarse meal. Gradually add 7 to 8 tablespoons cold water, tossing together with fork till all is moistened. Form into a ball. If desired, cover and chill for 1 hour.

Meanwhile, prepare meat filling. Combine beef, potatoes, turnip, onion, 1½ teaspoons salt, and pepper. Divide dough into 5 portions. For *each* pasty, roll one portion of dough on lightly floured surface to 9-inch circle. Place on ungreased baking sheet. Spoon *about 1 cup* filling on half of the circle; fold dough over filling to make a half-circle. Seal edges, using tines of fork; cut slits for escape of steam. Repeat with remaining dough and filling. Bake at 400° about 45 minutes.

In small saucepan combine catsup and ¼ cup water; heat through. Serve warm catsup sauce with meat pasties. Makes 5 servings.

Hardy and substantial midwestern foods pictured ▶ here are *Baking Powder Biscuits, Corn Relish, Pork-Applesauce-Kraut Bake, Lentil Soup, Best Tomato Catsup, Green Tomato Marmalade, Prune Kolacky, Mock Apple Pie, Chopped Beef Pasties,* and *Buckwheat Griddle Cakes.* (See Index for page numbers.)

Prune Kolacky

A sweet and spicy filled bun shown on page 21 —

    3½ to 4¼ cups all-purpose flour
    1 package active dry yeast
    ½ teaspoon grated lemon peel
    ¼ teaspoon ground nutmeg
    1 cup milk
    ⅓ cup sugar
    ⅓ cup shortening
    2 eggs
      Prune Filling

In large mixing bowl combine *2 cups* of the flour, yeast, peel, and nutmeg. Heat milk, sugar, shortening, and 1 teaspoon salt just till warm (115-120°), stirring constantly. Add to dry mixture; add eggs. Beat at low speed of electric mixer ½ minute; scrape sides of bowl constantly. Beat 3 minutes at high speed. Stir in *1¼ to 1¾ cups* flour to make a moderately soft dough. On floured surface knead in remaining ¼ to ½ cup flour; knead till smooth and elastic (5 to 8 minutes). Place in greased bowl; turn to grease surface. Cover; let rise till double (about 2 hours). Punch down; divide in half. Cover; let rest 10 minutes.

Shape *each* half into 12 balls; place 3 inches apart on greased baking sheets. Flatten *each* to 3-inch diameter. Cover; let rise till double (about 1 hour). Make depression in center of each; fill with Prune Filling. Bake at 375° for 10 to 12 minutes. Makes 24.

Prune Filling: Place 1½ cups dried prunes in saucepan with water to cover by 1 inch. Cover; bring to boiling. Simmer 25 to 30 minutes. Drain, pit, and chop; stir in ¼ cup sugar and ½ teaspoon ground cinnamon.

Baking Powder Biscuits

This popular quick bread is pictured on page 21 —

Combine 2 cups all-purpose flour, 1 tablespoon baking powder, and ½ teaspoon salt. Cut in ⅓ cup shortening till mixture resembles coarse crumbs. Make well in center; stir in ¾ cup milk just till dough clings together. Knead gently on floured surface (10 to 12 strokes); roll or pat to ½-inch thickness. Cut with 2½-inch biscuit cutter (do not twist); dip cutter in flour between cuts. Bake on ungreased baking sheet at 450° about 12 minutes. Makes 10.

Blueberry Sweet Rolls

    3¼ to 3½ cups all-purpose flour
    1 package active dry yeast
    2 5⅓-ounce cans evaporated milk
      (1⅓ cups)
    6 tablespoons butter *or* margarine
    ¼ cup sugar
    1 teaspoon salt
    1 egg
    6 tablespoons butter *or*
      margarine, melted
    ½ cup sugar
    2 teaspoons ground cinnamon
    1 teaspoon grated lemon peel
    2 cups fresh or frozen blueberries
      Confectioners' Icing

In large mixing bowl combine *1½ cups* of the flour and yeast. In saucepan heat milk, 6 tablespoons butter, ¼ cup sugar, and salt just till warm (115-120°), stirring constantly. Add to dry mixture; add egg. Beat at low speed of electric mixer ½ minute; scrape sides of bowl. Beat 3 minutes at high speed.

Stir in enough of the remaining flour to make a moderately stiff dough. Place in greased bowl; turn to grease surface. Cover; let rise till double (about 1½ hours). Punch down; divide in half. Cover; let rest 10 minutes.

On floured surface roll *half* of the dough to 14x8-inch rectangle; brush with *3 tablespoons* of the melted butter. Mix ½ cup sugar, cinnamon, and peel; sprinkle *half* of the mixture atop rectangle. Top with *1 cup* of the blueberries; press lightly into dough. Roll up jelly-roll fashion, starting with long side; seal edge. Repeat with remaining dough, melted butter, sugar mixture, and blueberries.

With knife, cut *each* roll into 12 slices. Or, cut rolls by placing a piece of regular or heavy-duty sewing thread under dough where you want to cut; pull ends of thread up around sides. Crisscross thread across top of roll and pull quickly as though tying a knot.

Place rolls in 2 greased 9x1½-inch round baking pans. Cover; let rise till double (about 30 minutes). Bake at 375° for 20 to 25 minutes. While warm, drizzle with Icing. Makes 24.

Confectioners' Icing: Stir together 1 cup sifted powdered sugar, ¼ teaspoon vanilla, and enough milk to make of drizzling consistency (about 1½ tablespoons).

Mock Apple Pie

Shown on page 21, this unusual pie was created by clever cooks who ran short of apples—

        Pastry for 2-crust 9-inch pie
    36 round cheese crackers
     2 cups sugar
     2 cups water
     2 teaspoons cream of tartar
     1 teaspoon shredded lemon peel
     2 tablespoons lemon juice
     2 tablespoons butter *or* margarine
        Ground cinnamon

Line 9-inch pie plate with pastry. Coarsely break crackers into pastry-lined pie plate. Combine sugar, water, and cream of tartar; bring to boiling. Boil gently, uncovered, 15 minutes. Remove from heat; stir in peel and juice. Cool. Pour over crackers. Dot with butter; sprinkle with cinnamon. Adjust top crust; cut slits for escape of steam. Bake at 425° till golden, 30 to 35 minutes. Serve warm.

Buckwheat Griddle Cakes

Hearty breakfast fare pictured on page 21—

     2⅔ cups all-purpose flour
     1⅓ cups buckwheat flour
     1 teaspoon salt
     1 package active dry yeast
     3 tablespoons packed brown sugar
     2 tablespoons cooking oil
     ¾ teaspoon baking soda

Mix flours and salt. Soften yeast in 2½ cups warm water (110°); stir in *1 tablespoon* of the sugar. Add to flour mixture; mix well. Cover; let stand overnight at room temperature. (Bowl must *not* be over half full.)

Next morning, stir the batter. Add remaining 2 tablespoons sugar, oil, and soda; mix well. Chill *1 cup* batter to use as starter (keeps several weeks). Bake remaining batter on hot, lightly greased griddle. Makes 16 large cakes.

To use starter: Place starter in large bowl; add 2¼ cups all-purpose flour, 2¼ cups water, and 1¼ cups buckwheat flour. Stir till smooth. Cover; let stand overnight as before. Next morning, stir. Add 2 tablespoons brown sugar, 2 tablespoons cooking oil, and ¾ teaspoon baking soda; mix well. Chill 1 cup batter to use as starter. Bake remaining batter as above.

Apple Cider Pie

This tangy fruit pie is shown on page 6—

     6 to 8 apples
     1 cup apple cider *or* apple juice
     ⅔ cup sugar
        Apple cider *or* apple juice
     2 tablespoons cornstarch
     1 teaspoon lemon juice
     1 teaspoon vanilla
     1 tablespoon butter *or* margarine
        Pastry for 9-inch
        lattice-top pie

Peel, core, and slice apples (6 cups). Bring 1 cup cider and sugar to boiling; add apples. Cook, uncovered, till tender, about 8 minutes. Drain; reserve syrup. If needed, add cider to syrup to equal 1⅓ cups. Mix cornstarch, lemon juice, vanilla, and 2 tablespoons cold water; stir with butter into syrup. Cook and stir till thickened and bubbly. Remove from heat; stir in apples. Line 9-inch pie plate with pastry; add apple mixture. Adjust lattice top; seal. Sprinkle with sugar, if desired. Bake at 400° till lightly browned, about 40 minutes.

Refrigerator Potato Rolls

A no-knead bread that you can mix ahead—

Peel and quarter 3 medium potatoes (1¼ pounds); cook in boiling salted water till tender, about 20 minutes. Drain. Mash to make 2 cups; do not add milk. In large mixing bowl combine 1½ cups all-purpose flour and 1 package active dry yeast. Heat 1 cup milk, ½ cup shortening, ⅓ cup sugar, and 1½ teaspoons salt just till warm (115-120°), stirring constantly. Remove from heat; stir in potatoes. Add to dry mixture; add 2 eggs. Beat at low speed of electric mixer ½ minute; scrape sides of bowl constantly. Beat 3 minutes at high speed. Stir in 3 cups all-purpose flour. Place dough in greased bowl; turn once to grease surface. Cover; chill for several hours or up to 3 or 4 days.

To use, divide dough in half. With floured hands, shape half of the dough into 16 rolls. Place in a greased 9x9x2-inch baking pan. Repeat with remaining dough. Cover; let rise in warm place till almost double (45 to 60 minutes). Bake at 375° for 30 to 35 minutes. Remove from pans; cool. Makes 32 rolls.

Salmon with Wild Rice

An impressive entrée shown on page 6 —

½ cup wild rice
1 13¾-ounce can chicken broth
1½ cups sliced fresh mushrooms
½ cup chopped celery
½ cup chopped onion
¼ cup chopped green pepper
¼ cup butter *or* margarine
1¼ cups regular rice
1 tablespoon Worcestershire sauce
1 teaspoon salt
⅛ teaspoon pepper
1 6-pound dressed salmon
Lemon
Cucumber slices

Rinse wild rice. In 2-quart saucepan bring chicken broth and 1 cup water to boiling; add wild rice. Reduce heat; cover and simmer 20 minutes. Meanwhile, cook mushrooms, celery, onion, and green pepper in butter till tender but not brown. Remove from heat; stir in regular rice, Worcestershire, salt, and pepper. Stir vegetable mixture into wild rice. Cook, covered, over low heat till rice is tender and liquid is absorbed, about 20 minutes more.

Rinse and pat fish dry; place in greased 15½x10½x1-inch baking pan. Sprinkle fish cavity with salt and pepper; stuff loosely with rice mixture.* Bake, covered, at 350° till fish flakes easily with fork, about 1½ hours. Serve with lemon and cucumber. If desired, trim with parsley and/or curly endive. Serves 12.

*Spoon remaining stuffing into greased 1-quart casserole; add 2 tablespoons water. Bake, covered, at 350° about 30 minutes.

Blackberry Pie

1¼ cups sugar
¼ cup all-purpose flour
2 tablespoons cornstarch
⅛ teaspoon salt
4 cups blackberries
Pastry for 2-crust 9-inch pie

Combine sugar, flour, cornstarch, and salt; toss with blackberries. Line 9-inch pie plate with pastry; fill with berry mixture. Adjust top crust; seal. Cut slits for escape of steam. Bake at 400° for 40 to 45 minutes.

Lingcod Chowder

1 pound fresh *or* frozen
lingcod steaks
1 bay leaf
¼ teaspoon dried thyme, crushed
4 slices bacon
½ cup chopped onion
½ cup sliced celery
2 cups diced, peeled, raw potatoes
2 cups shredded sharp American
cheese (8 ounces)
3 cups milk
¼ cup snipped parsley
2 tablespoons chopped
canned pimiento
3 tablespoons all-purpose flour

In large saucepan bring first 3 ingredients and 1½ cups water to boiling; reduce heat and simmer till fish flakes easily with fork, 15 to 20 minutes. Cool. Remove skin and bones from fish. Break fish into chunks; set aside. Strain broth; reserve. In same saucepan cook bacon till crisp. Remove bacon and crumble; set aside. In bacon drippings cook onion and celery till tender. Stir in reserved broth and potatoes. Cook, covered, till potatoes are just tender, 10 to 15 minutes; stir occasionally. Stir in cheese till melted. Add fish, milk, parsley, pimiento, reserved bacon, 1 teaspoon salt, and ⅛ teaspoon pepper. Stir ⅓ cup water into flour; stir into chowder. Cook and stir till thick and bubbly. Serves 6 to 8.

Layered Filbert Bars

Put ⅔ cup whole filberts (3 ounces) through food grinder, using coarse blade. Cream together ½ cup sifted powdered sugar, 6 tablespoons butter, 2 egg yolks, and ½ teaspoon salt. Stir in 1 cup all-purpose flour and ½ *cup* of nuts. Press into ungreased 9x9x2-inch baking pan. Bake at 350° for 15 to 20 minutes.

Combine ¼ cup blackberry jelly and ⅛ teaspoon ground cinnamon; spread over baked layer. Beat 2 egg whites till soft peaks form. Slowly add ⅓ cup granulated sugar; beat till stiff peaks form. Carefully spread over jelly layer. Sprinkle with remaining nuts. Bake at 350° for 15 to 20 minutes. Cool slightly; cut into bars while warm. Makes 24.

Rich and cheesy *Lingcod Chowder* and delicately flavored *Dungeness Crab au Gratin* are favorites in the Northwest, where fresh fish and seafood are readily available. The seasoning in these and similar dishes is kept subtle so as not to mask the delicate flavor of the fish or seafood.

Dungeness Crab au Gratin

        6 tablespoons butter *or* margarine
    ⅓ cup all-purpose flour
    ½ teaspoon salt
    ½ teaspoon grated lemon peel
    ¼ teaspoon dry mustard
        Dash white pepper
        1 beaten egg
        2 cups light cream
    3¼ pounds dungeness crab, cooked,
            shelled, and flaked
            (2½ cups crab meat)
        3 tablespoons sliced green onion
        1 cup soft bread crumbs
    ½ cup shredded Swiss cheese
    ¼ cup sliced almonds, toasted

In saucepan melt *4 tablespoons* of the butter or margarine; blend in flour, salt, peel, mustard, and pepper. Mix egg and cream; add to flour mixture all at once. Cook and stir over medium heat till thickened; do not boil. Stir in crab and onion. Pour into 4 individual 1-cup casseroles. Bake at 350° for 15 minutes. Melt remaining 2 tablespoons butter; toss with crumbs, cheese, and almonds. Sprinkle around edge of casseroles; bake till cheese melts, about 5 minutes longer. Makes 4 servings.

Northern Bean Salad

        1 cup dry northern beans
        1 tablespoon tarragon vinegar
    ½ teaspoon salt
    ½ teaspoon dry mustard
        1 small clove garlic, minced
            Dash bottled hot pepper sauce
        2 tablespoons salad oil
    ¼ cup chopped onion
    ¼ cup chopped green pepper
    ¼ cup chopped dill pickle
        2 tablespoons snipped parsley
    ⅓ cup mayonnaise *or* salad
            dressing
    ⅓ cup dairy sour cream

Rinse beans. In saucepan bring beans and 3 cups water to boiling; reduce heat. Boil 2 minutes; remove from heat. Cover; let stand 1 hour. (Or, soak beans in 3 cups water overnight.) Bring to boiling; reduce heat. Simmer, covered, till just tender but not broken, 40 to 50 minutes. Drain well. Mix vinegar with next 4 ingredients; beat in oil till smooth and thick. Pour over beans; cover. Chill overnight. Combine bean mixture, onion, green pepper, pickle, and parsley; add mayonnaise and sour cream. Toss gently; chill. Serves 6.

Western-Style Cooking

The sunny climate of the Far West provides a year-round supply of fresh fruits and vegetables. In addition, California is especially famous for its sourdough bread and abalone.

Southwestern cooks use fiery spices to make enchiladas, tacos, tamales, and chilies rellenos. Texas cooks also prepare Mexican-style dishes, but they are equally noted for barbecued foods, often made in ample amounts to serve a crowd.

Texas Sheet Cake

Chocolaty and moist with a hint of cinnamon—

- 1 cup water
- ½ cup butter *or* margarine
- ¼ cup shortening
- ¼ cup unsweetened cocoa powder
- 2 cups all-purpose flour
- 2 cups granulated sugar
- 1 teaspoon baking soda
- 1 teaspoon ground cinnamon
- ½ teaspoon salt
- ½ cup buttermilk
- 2 eggs
- 1 teaspoon vanilla
- ½ cup butter *or* margarine
- 6 tablespoons buttermilk
- ¼ cup unsweetened cocoa powder
- 1 16-ounce package powdered
  sugar, sifted (about 4¾ cups)
- 1 teaspoon vanilla

In saucepan combine water, ½ cup butter or margarine, shortening, and ¼ cup cocoa powder; cook and stir till boiling. Remove from heat.

In mixing bowl stir together flour, granulated sugar, baking soda, cinnamon, and salt. Add hot cocoa mixture; mix till smooth. Add ½ cup buttermilk, eggs, and 1 teaspoon vanilla; beat well. Pour into greased 15½x10½x1-inch baking pan. Bake at 375° for 20 minutes.

Meanwhile, in saucepan combine ½ cup butter, 6 tablespoons buttermilk, and ¼ cup cocoa powder. Cook and stir till boiling; remove from heat. Gradually blend in powdered sugar and 1 teaspoon vanilla till smooth. Immediately pour frosting over warm cake. Cool.

Herbed Lamb Kabobs

Mix ½ cup cooking oil; ½ cup chopped onion; ¼ cup snipped parsley; ¼ cup lemon juice; 1 teaspoon salt; 1 teaspoon dried marjoram, crushed; 1 teaspoon dried thyme, crushed; 1 clove garlic, minced; and ½ teaspoon pepper. Stir in 2 pounds boneless lamb, cut in 1-inch cubes. Cover; chill overnight, stirring occasionally. Drain; reserve marinade. Cook wedges of onion in water; drain. Thread skewers with meat, precooked onion wedges, green pepper squares, and sweet red pepper squares. Broil over *hot* coals 10 to 12 minutes; turn and brush often with marinade. Makes 6 servings.

Sopaipillas

Pillow-shaped fritters shown on page 6—

- 2 cups all-purpose flour
- 1 tablespoon baking powder
- 1 tablespoon shortening
  Fat for frying
- 1 cup sugar
- 4 teaspoons ground cinnamon

Stir together flour, baking powder, and ½ teaspoon salt; cut in shortening till mixture resembles cornmeal. Gradually add ⅔ cup lukewarm water, stirring with fork; dough will be crumbly. On lightly floured surface knead till a smooth ball is formed. Divide in half; let stand 10 minutes. Roll *each* half to 12½x10-inch rectangle. Cut in 2½-inch squares. *Do not reroll.* Fry 3 or 4 at a time in deep hot fat (400°), about 30 seconds on *each* side. Drain on paper toweling. Roll in mixture of sugar and ground cinnamon. Makes 40.

This round-up of western foods is hearty enough to ▶ satisfy even a ranch-hand's appetite. Included are a fresh *Fruit Salad Platter* topped with a choice of dressing, brownie-like *Texas Sheet Cake*, generous slices of *Sourdough Bread,* and western-style *Herbed Lamb Kabobs.* (See Index for page numbers.)

Fruit Salad Platter

A bountiful array of fresh fruits with a variety of dressings shown on page 27—

    2 large bananas
    1 papaya
    ¼ cup orange juice
      Lettuce
    1 pineapple, peeled, eyes
        removed, cored, and
        cut in spears
    2 cups honeydew melon balls
    1 cantaloupe, peeled and sliced
    1 pint strawberries
      Mint sprigs
        • • •
      Honey-Lime Dressing
      Spicy Nectar Dressing
      Strawberry-Cheese Dressing

Chill fruits, except bananas. Peel and slice bananas and papaya; add orange juice. Stir to coat. On large lettuce-lined platter arrange banana slices, papaya, pineapple spears, honeydew balls, cantaloupe slices, and strawberries. Garnish with mint. Serve with Honey-Lime Dressing, Spicy Nectar Dressing, and Strawberry-Cheese Dressing. Makes 8 servings.

Honey-Lime Dressing: In small mixing bowl blend together ½ cup honey, ¼ teaspoon grated lime peel, ¼ cup lime juice, ¼ teaspoon salt, and ¼ teaspoon ground mace. Gradually add ¾ cup salad oil, beating with electric mixer or rotary beater till mixture is thickened. Beat in 2 drops green food coloring. Cover and chill thoroughly. Makes 1½ cups dressing.

Spicy Nectar Dressing: In small mixing bowl combine 1 cup dairy sour cream, ½ cup apricot nectar, ½ cup salad oil, 3 tablespoons sugar, ½ teaspoon ground cinnamon, ½ teaspoon paprika, and dash salt. Beat ingredients together with electric mixer or rotary beater till mixture is smooth. Cover dressing and chill thoroughly. Makes 1¾ cups dressing.

Strawberry-Cheese Dressing: In small mixing bowl beat together one 3-ounce package softened cream cheese; ½ of a 10-ounce package frozen strawberries, thawed (½ cup); 1 tablespoon sugar; 1 tablespoon lemon juice; and dash salt. Gradually add ½ cup salad oil, beating till mixture is thickened. Beat in 1 to 2 drops red food coloring. Cover and chill thoroughly. Makes 1⅓ cups dressing.

Mustard Barbecued Ribs

These ribs, trimmed with chili peppers, onion, and parsley, are shown on page 6—

Sprinkle 4 pounds pork spareribs with salt. Place ribs, meaty side down, in shallow roasting pan. Roast, uncovered, at 450° for 30 minutes; drain. Turn ribs meaty side up. Reduce oven to 350°; roast, uncovered, 1 hour more. Drain again. (Or, omit salting and oven-roasting; cut ribs into serving pieces. Cover with salted water; simmer, covered, till tender, about 1 hour. Drain.) Place oven-cooked ribs or simmered ribs in shallow roasting pan. Spoon some of the Barbecue Sauce over ribs. Roast, uncovered, at 350° for 30 minutes; baste occasionally with sauce. Serves 4.

Barbecue Sauce: In saucepan combine ½ cup catsup; ¼ cup water; ¼ cup finely chopped onion; 3 tablespoons red wine vinegar; 2 tablespoons cooking oil; 2 teaspoons packed brown sugar; 2 teaspoons Worcestershire sauce; 2 teaspoons whole mustard seed; 1 teaspoon paprika; ½ teaspoon dried oregano, crushed; ½ teaspoon chili powder; ¼ teaspoon salt; ⅛ teaspoon ground cloves; 1 bay leaf; and 1 clove garlic, minced. Simmer, uncovered, 10 minutes, stirring once or twice. Discard bay leaf.

Western Tossed Salad

Mixed greens combo shown on page 6—

    2 cups torn lettuce
    2 cups torn romaine
    2 cups torn curly endive
    1 cup drained garbanzo beans
   12 cherry tomatoes, halved
    ⅓ cup sliced pitted ripe olives
    ¼ cup sliced green onion with tops
      Western Dressing
    1 large avocado

In salad bowl combine first 7 ingredients. Pour Western Dressing over all; toss lightly. Halve, pit, and peel avocado; slice. Arrange avocado slices atop salad. Makes 6 servings.

Western Dressing: In screw top jar combine ⅔ cup salad oil; ⅓ cup tarragon vinegar; 1 clove garlic, minced; 1 teaspoon sugar; ½ teaspoon *each* salt, onion powder, dry mustard, and paprika; ¼ teaspoon celery salt; and few drops bottled hot pepper sauce. Cover; shake.

Sourdough Bread

This specialty bread is pictured on page 27 —

To make Sourdough Starter: In bowl soften 1 package active dry yeast in ½ cup *warm* water (110°). Stir in 2 cups *warm* water, 2 cups all-purpose flour, and 1 tablespoon sugar. Beat till smooth. Cover with cheesecloth. Let stand at room temperature till bubbly, 5 to 10 days; stir 2 or 3 times a day. (Fermentation time depends on room temperature; a warmer room will hasten the process.) Store Starter covered, in refrigerator. To use, bring desired amount to room temperature.

    1 package active dry yeast
    1½ cups warm water (110°)
    5½ to 6 cups all-purpose flour
    1 cup Sourdough Starter (room
        temperature)
    2 teaspoons salt
    2 teaspoons sugar
    ½ teaspoon baking soda

To make bread: In large mixing bowl soften yeast in warm water. Blend in *2½ cups* of the flour, Sourdough Starter, salt, and sugar. Combine *2½ cups* of the flour and baking soda; stir into flour-yeast mixture. Add enough remaining flour to make a stiff dough. Turn out onto lightly floured surface; knead till smooth and elastic (5 to 7 minutes). Shape dough into a ball. Place in greased bowl, turning once to grease surface. Cover dough and let rise in warm place till double (about 1½ hours). Punch down; divide dough in half.

Cover and let rest 10 minutes. Shape *each* half into a round loaf. Place loaves on lightly greased baking sheets. With sharp knife, make parallel slashes across tops of loaves. Let rise in warm place till loaves are double (1 to 1½ hours). Bake at 400° for 35 to 40 minutes. Remove bread from baking pans; cool on wire rack. If desired, brush loaves with butter or margarine. Makes 2 loaves.

To keep Starter going: After using some Starter, stir ¾ cup water, ¾ cup all-purpose flour, and 1 teaspoon sugar into remaining Starter. Let stand at room temperature till bubbly, at least 1 day. Cover Starter and refrigerate for later use. If not used within 10 days, stir 1 teaspoon sugar into Starter. Keep adding sugar every 10 days.

Chicken Enchiladas

    2 whole large chicken breasts,
        halved lengthwise
    1 cup chopped onion
    1 clove garlic, minced
    2 tablespoons butter *or* margarine
    1 16-ounce can tomatoes, cut up
    1 8-ounce can tomato sauce
    ¼ cup chopped canned
        green chili peppers
    1 teaspoon sugar
    1 teaspoon ground cumin
    ½ teaspoon dried oregano, crushed
    ½ teaspoon dried basil, crushed
    12 Corn Tortillas (see recipe
        below or purchase tortillas)
    2½ cups shredded Monterey Jack
        cheese (10 ounces)
    ¾ cup dairy sour cream

Simmer chicken in water to cover till tender, 15 to 20 minutes. Drain; carefully remove skin and bones. Sprinkle chicken with a little salt. Cut into 12 strips; set aside.

In saucepan cook onion and garlic in butter till tender. Add undrained tomatoes, next 6 ingredients, and ½ teaspoon salt. Bring to boiling; reduce heat. Simmer, covered, 20 minutes; remove from heat. Dip *each* tortilla in hot sauce to soften. On *each,* place *one* chicken strip and about *2 tablespoons* of the cheese; roll up. Place, seam side down, in 13x9x2-inch baking dish. Blend sour cream into remaining sauce; pour over tortillas. Sprinkle with remaining cheese. Cover; bake at 350° till hot, about 40 minutes. Serves 6.

Corn Tortillas

In mixing bowl combine 2 cups corn flour (masa harina) and 1 cup water; mix well with hands. Add more water, if needed. (Dough should be moist, but should hold its shape.) Divide into 12 balls. Dampen balls slightly with water; press *each* ball between 2 sheets of waxed paper, using a tortilla press or flat baking dish. Gently peel off top paper. Place tortilla, paper side up, on hot ungreased griddle. Gently peel off remaining paper. Cook tortilla till edges begin to dry, about 30 seconds. Turn; cook till puffs appear. Makes 12.

Oxtail Stew

⅓ cup all-purpose flour
1 teaspoon salt
3 pounds oxtails, cut in
    2½-inch pieces
2 tablespoons cooking oil
6 carrots, cut in 1-inch pieces
1 cup chopped onion
1 cup chopped celery
1 clove garlic, minced
2½ cups beef broth
2 tablespoons tomato paste
1 bay leaf, broken
¼ teaspoon dried thyme, crushed

Mix flour, salt, and ¼ teaspoon pepper; coat oxtails in flour mixture. In Dutch oven brown the oxtails, half at a time, in hot oil. Remove oxtails; drain, reserving 2 tablespoons oil. In reserved oil cook carrots, onion, celery, and garlic till onion and celery are tender. Add remaining ingredients; bring to boiling. Add oxtails. Cover; simmer till tender, 2 to 2½ hours. Skim off fat. Makes 4 servings.

Hangtown Fry

6 eggs
⅓ cup milk
½ teaspoon salt
¼ cup all-purpose flour
½ teaspoon salt
    Dash pepper
12 medium-sized shucked oysters
2 tablespoons butter *or* margarine
3 or 4 slices bacon, cooked
    and drained

Beat eggs with milk and ½ teaspoon salt. Mix flour, remaining ½ teaspoon salt, and pepper. Roll oysters in seasoned flour till coated. In skillet melt butter or margarine. Cook oysters in butter till edges curl, about 1 minute on *each* side. Pour egg mixture into skillet with oysters. As egg mixture begins to set on bottom and sides, lift and fold over with wide spatula. Cook till eggs are cooked throughout, 4 to 5 minutes. Remove from heat; garnish with bacon strips. Serve immediately. Makes 3 or 4 servings.

The bold flavor of western-style cooking is found in *Oxtail Stew* (top, left), *Barbecued Short Ribs*, *Sourdough Bread* (see recipe, page 29), *Beef Flautas* with *Avocado Sauce, Spanish Steak,* and *Chilies Rellenos.* Also shown is *Hangtown Fry,* a dish popular during California gold rush days.

Chilies Rellenos

    3 peeled canned green chili
        peppers *or* fresh long green
        hot peppers
    1 to 1½ cups shredded Cheddar
        cheese (4 to 6 ounces)
    All-purpose flour
    6 egg whites
    6 egg yolks
    3 tablespoons all-purpose flour
    Fat for frying

Halve chili peppers crosswise. (To prepare fresh peppers, place on baking sheet in 450° oven till skins form black blisters, about 15 minutes, giving a quarter-turn once. Peppers will be cooked. Cool slightly; peel. Carefully remove stems and seeds; halve crosswise.) Stuff peppers with cheese; coat with a little flour.

Beat egg whites till stiff but not dry peaks form. To yolks add 3 tablespoons flour and ¼ teaspoon salt; beat till thick and lemon-colored. Fold yolk mixture into whites.

For *each* pepper, spoon about ⅓ cup egg batter into ½ inch hot fat (375°) in skillet; spread into a circle. As batter begins to set, gently top each mound with a stuffed pepper. Cover with another ⅓ cup batter; cook till underside is browned, 2 to 3 minutes. Turn carefully; brown other side. Drain on paper toweling. Serve at once. Makes 6 servings.

Spanish Steak

    ¼ cup all-purpose flour
    2 pounds beef round steak, cut in
        6 serving-size pieces
    2 tablespoons cooking oil
    1 16-ounce can tomatoes, cut up
    1 15½-ounce can dark red kidney
        beans, drained
    ¼ cup chopped green pepper
    2 tablespoons vinegar
    1 tablespoon sugar
    1 teaspoon chili powder
    ½ teaspoon ground cumin

Pound flour into meat; brown meat in hot oil. Drain off excess fat. Combine undrained tomatoes, remaining ingredients, and 1 teaspoon salt; pour over meat. Cover; simmer till tender, 45 to 50 minutes. Makes 6 servings.

Beef Flautas

    2 cups thinly sliced cooked beef
        strips (about 12 ounces)
    1 tablespoon cooking oil
    1 tablespoon red wine vinegar
    1½ teaspoons chili powder
    ½ teaspoon salt
    ½ teaspoon dried oregano, crushed
    ⅛ teaspoon garlic powder
    Cooking oil
    12 Corn Tortillas (see recipe on
        page 29 or purchase tortillas)
    Avocado Sauce

Brown the meat in 1 tablespoon hot oil; drain. Add vinegar, chili powder, salt, oregano, and garlic powder to meat; toss. Set aside.

Pour oil 1 inch deep into 2-quart saucepan; heat. Dip *each* tortilla in hot oil just till soft and limp but not browned, about 5 seconds; drain well on paper toweling.

To assemble flautas, divide beef among tortillas, placing a few strips at one edge of *each* tortilla. Starting at filled edge, roll up tightly; secure with wooden pick. Fry in hot oil in saucepan till crisp, about 2 minutes. Lift carefully from oil; drain well. Serve with Avocado Sauce. Makes 4 to 6 servings.

Avocado Sauce: Grate enough lemon peel to make ½ teaspoon; set aside. Blend ½ cup mashed ripe avocado (1 medium avocado) with 1 teaspoon lemon juice and ¼ teaspoon salt. Stir in ½ cup dairy sour cream; top with lemon peel.

Barbecued Short Ribs

    4 pounds beef short ribs
    ⅔ cup catsup
    ¼ cup light molasses
    ¼ cup lemon juice
    1 tablespoon dry mustard
    ½ teaspoon chili powder
    Dash garlic powder

Trim excess fat from ribs; season with salt and pepper. Place ribs in Dutch oven; add water to cover. Simmer, covered, till tender, about 2 hours. Drain; place ribs on rack of broiler pan. Combine catsup and remaining ingredients; brush over ribs. Broil 4 to 5 inches from heat for 10 to 15 minutes; turn often, basting with sauce. Makes 4 servings.

Good Old-Fashioned Recipes

Many of the dishes in this chapter may look similar to foods you remember enjoying as a child— and they should. They are adaptations of old-time recipes that have been cherished for years.

Glance through the next few pages for a tempting array of slow-cooking pot roasts, stews, and soups. Following these, you'll find salad and vegetable recipes from early days that turn the garden produce into succulent dishes. And don't overlook the mouth-watering collection of breads, desserts, and candies that were—and still are—a part of every cook's repertoire.

Also included in this section are family-type recipes suitable for packing and toting to church suppers, potlucks, and picnics.

Nothing whets the appetite like good home cooking. Favorites sure to be winners at your dinner table are *Corn and Rice Especiale, Hearty Vegetable Soup, Raspberry-Pear Cobbler, Cinnamon Rolls,* and *Fruit-Glazed Corned Beef.* (See Index for page numbers.)

Main Dishes from the Past

Are you looking for recipes reminiscent of some of the full-flavored meat dishes you remember as a child? On the following pages you'll find a sampling of pot roasts, meat pies, casseroles, skillet dishes, stuffed meats, stews, and soups—all made with everyday ingredients. Although many of the recipes take time to prepare, the end result is well worth the effort.

Stuffed Turkey Loaf

    2 beaten eggs
    1 5⅓-ounce can evaporated milk
    ⅓ cup chicken broth
    1½ cups soft bread crumbs
        (2 slices bread)
    ⅔ cup finely chopped celery
    2 tablespoons chopped
        canned pimiento
    ½ teaspoon salt
      Dash pepper
      Dash ground nutmeg
      Dash dried rosemary, crushed
    4 cups coarsely ground cooked
        turkey
      Rice Stuffing
      Mushroom Sauce

Combine eggs, evaporated milk, chicken broth, bread crumbs, celery, pimiento, salt, pepper, nutmeg, and rosemary. Add ground turkey; mix thoroughly. Pat *half* of the turkey mixture into 8x8x2-inch baking pan. Spread Rice Stuffing over meat; pat in remaining turkey mixture. Bake at 350° till center of loaf is firm, about 45 minutes. Cut into squares; serve with Mushroom Sauce. Makes 6 servings.

Rice Stuffing: In saucepan cook ½ cup brown rice in 1 cup chicken broth, covered, till tender, about 45 minutes. Cook ¼ cup chopped onion in 2 tablespoons butter *or* margarine till tender but not brown. Combine rice, onion, 1 beaten egg, and ½ teaspoon rubbed sage.

Mushroom Sauce: In saucepan stir 1 cup dairy sour cream into one 10¾-ounce can condensed cream of mushroom soup. Add 1 teaspoon paprika; cook and stir till hot. *Do not boil.*

Chicken and Dumplings

    1 5- to 6-pound ready-to-cook
        stewing chicken, cut up, *or*
    2 3-pound ready-to-cook
        broiler-fryer chickens, cut up
    4 stalks celery with leaves,
        cut up
    1 carrot, sliced
    1 small onion, cut up
    2 sprigs parsley
    1 bay leaf
    2 teaspoons salt
    ¼ teaspoon pepper
      Homemade Dumplings
    ½ cup all-purpose flour
    1½ teaspoons salt
    ⅛ teaspoon pepper

In Dutch oven or large kettle add water to chicken to cover. Add celery and next 6 ingredients. Cover; bring to boiling. Reduce heat; simmer till meat is tender, about 2½ hours.

Prepare Homemade Dumplings; drop from tablespoon *directly onto chicken* in boiling stock. Cover tightly; return to boiling. Reduce heat; *do not lift cover.* Simmer 12 to 15 minutes.

Remove dumplings and chicken to platter; keep hot. Strain broth. In saucepan bring 4 cups broth to boiling. Stir 1 cup cold water into flour; gradually add to broth, mixing well. Cook and stir till thick and bubbly. Stir in 1½ teaspoons salt and ⅛ teaspoon pepper. Pour over chicken and dumplings. Serves 6 to 8.

Homemade Dumplings: Stir 1 cup all-purpose flour with 2 teaspoons baking powder and ½ teaspoon salt. Mix ½ cup milk and 2 tablespoons cooking oil; add with 2 tablespoons snipped parsley to flour mixture. Stir to moisten.

Home cooking is a platter of *Chicken and Dumplings* dressed in a smooth and golden gravy. To make this specialty dish from Grandmother's days, simmer the chicken till tender, then top with parsley-flecked dumplings and steam till light and fluffy. Strain and thicken the well-seasoned broth for gravy. ▶

Spaghetti Skillet Pie

6 ounces spaghetti
2 tablespoons butter *or* margarine
2 beaten eggs
⅓ cup grated Parmesan cheese
1 pound bulk pork sausage
½ cup chopped onion
¼ cup chopped green pepper
1 8-ounce can tomatoes, cut up
1 6-ounce can tomato paste
1 teaspoon sugar
1 teaspoon dried oregano, crushed
½ teaspoon garlic salt
1 12-ounce carton cream-style
    cottage cheese (1½ cups)
½ cup shredded mozzarella
    cheese (2 ounces)

Cook spaghetti following package directions; drain. (Should have 3¼ cups.) Stir butter into hot spaghetti; stir in eggs and Parmesan.

In 12-inch non-stick* electric skillet cook sausage, onion, and green pepper till meat is browned and vegetables are tender; drain. Stir in undrained tomatoes and next 4 ingredients; heat through. Remove meat sauce from skillet; turn skillet off. Wipe with damp paper towel.

In same skillet* put spaghetti in layer to form a "crust." Spread cottage cheese over bottom of spaghetti crust. Fill "pie" with meat sauce. Cover; bake with skillet set at 250° (low), about 20 minutes. Sprinkle mozzarella over pie. Bake, covered, 5 minutes. Serves 6.

*If electric skillet does not have non-stick surface, spray with non-stick cooking spray.

Corn-Stuffed Pork Chops

This man-pleasing entrée is pictured on page 4—

Cook 1 cup chopped celery and ½ cup chopped onion in ¼ cup butter till tender. Combine celery mixture; 4 cups slightly dry soft bread crumbs (6 slices bread); one 8¾-ounce can whole kernel corn, undrained; ½ teaspoon salt; ½ teaspoon rubbed sage; and dash pepper. Season 12 thinly sliced pork chops with salt and pepper. Place 6 chops on rack in shallow baking pan. Spoon about ½ cup of the stuffing atop *each;* top *each* with one of the remaining chops. Cover with foil; bake at 325° till tender, about 1¼ hours. Sprinkle with paprika. Serves 6.

Beefy Garbanzo Casserole

In saucepan cook 1 pound ground beef; 1 cup chopped onion; and 2 cloves garlic, minced, till beef is browned and onion is tender. Drain. Stir in two 15-ounce cans garbanzo beans, drained; one 15-ounce can tomato sauce; ½ cup water; 1 teaspoon dried oregano, crushed; ½ teaspoon salt; ½ teaspoon ground cumin; ¼ teaspoon pepper; and 2 bay leaves. Heat mixture to boiling. Turn into 1½-quart casserole. Bake, covered, at 350° for 45 minutes. Remove bay leaves; stir. Garnish with onion rings, if desired. Makes 5 or 6 servings.

Pork Pie Dinner

1½ pounds boneless lean pork, cut
    in 1-inch cubes (3½ cups)
½ cup chopped onion
1 teaspoon ground sage
¾ teaspoon salt
    Cheese Pastry
½ cup milk
¼ cup all-purpose flour
2 large tart apples, peeled,
    cored, and thinly sliced
1 tablespoon sugar

In 3-quart saucepan brown the pork over medium-high heat. Add onion, sage, salt, and 1 cup water. Simmer, covered, till pork is tender, about 20 minutes. Prepare Cheese Pastry. Stir milk into flour; stir into pork. Cook and stir till thickened and bubbly. Turn *half* of the hot pork into casserole lined with Cheese Pastry. Place apples over meat; sprinkle with sugar. Top with remaining pork; arrange pastry wedges atop meat. Bake at 450° for 10 minutes. Reduce oven to 350°; bake 25 minutes more. Garnish with parsley, if desired. Makes 6 servings.

Cheese Pastry: Stir 1 cup all-purpose flour with ¼ teaspoon salt; add ⅔ cup shredded sharp Cheddar cheese. Toss well with fork. Cut in ⅓ cup shortening with pastry blender till pieces are size of small peas. Sprinkle 1 tablespoon cold water over part of mixture; toss with fork and push to side. Repeat with 2 more tablespoons cold water. Form into ball. Roll ⅔ of the pastry to 11-inch circle. Line 1½-quart casserole with pastry. Roll remaining pastry to 6½-inch circle; cut into 6 wedges.

Lamb Shanks and Lentils

 6 medium lamb shanks (about 8
  ounces each)
 2 tablespoons cooking oil
 2 cloves garlic, minced
 ½ teaspoon dried thyme, crushed
  Dash pepper
 1½ cups dry lentils, rinsed
 3 whole cloves
 1 small onion
 ½ cup chopped carrot
 1 bay leaf
 6 thin slices lemon

In large skillet brown the shanks in hot oil. Add garlic, thyme, pepper, ½ cup water, and ½ teaspoon salt. Cover; cook over low heat 1 hour.

In medium saucepan combine lentils and 3 cups water. Insert cloves in onion; add to lentils with carrot, bay leaf, and 1½ teaspoons salt. Simmer, covered, till vegetables are tender, 50 to 60 minutes. Spoon vegetables into 12x7½x2-inch baking dish. Top with lamb shanks and lemon slices. Bake, covered, at 350° for 30 to 35 minutes. Discard onion and bay leaf; stir before serving. Makes 6 servings.

Salmon-Rice Pie

  Pastry for 2-crust 9-inch pie
 1 16-ounce can salmon, drained
 2 cups cooked rice
 ½ cup milk
 2 hard-cooked eggs, chopped
 2 tablespoons snipped parsley
 ½ cup chopped onion
 2 tablespoons butter *or* margarine
  Cheese Sauce

Line 9-inch pie plate with pastry. Flake salmon; combine with rice, milk, eggs, parsley, and ¼ teaspoon salt. Set aside. Cook onion in butter till tender; stir into rice mixture. Turn into pastry shell. Cover with top crust. Cut slits for escape of steam. Bake at 375° for 45 minutes. Serve with Cheese Sauce. Makes 6 servings.

Cheese Sauce: Melt 2 tablespoons butter *or* margarine; stir in 2 tablespoons all-purpose flour and ¼ teaspoon salt. Add 1¼ cups milk; cook and stir till thickened and bubbly. Stir in ½ cup shredded American cheese and ½ cup shredded Swiss cheese till melted.

Lamb-Vegetable Supper

 1 pound boneless lamb, cut in
  1-inch cubes
 2 tablespoons all-purpose flour
 3 tablespoons cooking oil
 1 clove garlic, minced
 1 bay leaf
 ½ teaspoon dried basil, crushed
 ¼ teaspoon dried thyme, crushed
 4 medium potatoes, peeled and
  quartered (1½ pounds)
 3 carrots, cut in ¾-inch pieces
 2 onions, cut in eighths
 1 tomato

Coat lamb with flour. In heavy 3-quart saucepan brown the lamb, half at a time, in hot oil. Drain. Add garlic, bay leaf, basil, thyme, 2½ cups water, 1½ teaspoons salt, and ⅛ teaspoon pepper. Simmer, covered, 30 minutes.

Add potatoes, carrots, and onions; simmer, covered, till vegetables are tender, about 20 minutes. Peel tomato; cut into 6 wedges. Add to stew; cook, covered, till heated through, 2 to 3 minutes. Remove bay leaf. Serves 4.

Shaker Beef Goulash

A meal-in-one stew topped with mashed potatoes—

Cut 1 pound beef stew meat into 1-inch cubes. In paper or plastic bag combine 1 tablespoon all-purpose flour, 1 teaspoon salt, and dash pepper; add beef cubes, a few at a time, shaking to coat with flour mixture. In large saucepan brown the beef in 1 tablespoon hot cooking oil. Add 1 medium onion, sliced; 1 cup water; and ½ cup apple juice. Cover and simmer till meat is tender, about 1½ hours.

To meat mixture add 1 medium rutabaga, peeled and diced (about 2 cups); 3 large carrots, diced (about 1 cup); 1 cup water; 1 tablespoon snipped parsley; ¾ teaspoon salt; ⅛ teaspoon dried marjoram, crushed; and ⅛ teaspoon dried thyme, crushed. Simmer, covered, till vegetables are tender, about 30 minutes.

Stir ¼ cup cold water into 2 tablespoons all-purpose flour; stir into meat mixture. Cook and stir till mixture is thickened and bubbly. Transfer stew to serving dish; spoon 4 or 5 servings of hot mashed potatoes around edge of stew. Makes 4 or 5 servings.

Slow, moist cooking is the secret to serving a delectable main dish such as *Savory Blade Pot Roast*. Prepared from a less-tender cut of meat, this pot roast simmers to a juicy doneness in a simple, yet distinctive sauce made with catsup, wine vinegar, soy, Worcestershire sauce, and rosemary.

Savory Blade Pot Roast

    1 3-pound beef blade roast
    1 tablespoon cooking oil
      Salt
         • • •
    ¼ cup wine vinegar
    ¼ cup catsup
    ¼ cup water
    2 tablespoons soy sauce
    2 tablespoons Worcestershire
      sauce
    1 teaspoon dried rosemary
    ½ teaspoon garlic powder
    ½ teaspoon dry mustard

Brown the meat slowly in hot oil; remove from heat. Drain; sprinkle meat with salt. Combine vinegar and remaining ingredients; pour over meat. Return to heat. Cover tightly; simmer till tender, 1½ to 1¾ hours. Remove meat to serving platter. Skim excess fat from pan juices; spoon juices over meat. Makes 6 to 8 servings.

Beef and Bean Pot Roast

Vegetable-sauced roast shown on the cover —

    1 3-pound beef chuck roast
    2 tablespoons cooking oil
    1 cup chopped onion
    1 cup dry lima beans, rinsed
    ½ cup catsup
    1 teaspoon salt
    ⅛ teaspoon pepper
    1 clove garlic, minced
    2 teaspoons mixed pickling spice
    5 carrots, sliced (about 1½ cups)

In Dutch oven brown the meat in hot oil; remove meat. Drain off fat. In same Dutch oven combine onion, next 5 ingredients, and 2 cups water. Tie pickling spice in cheesecloth bag; add to beans. Place meat atop beans. Simmer, covered, till meat and beans are almost tender, about 2 hours. (Add water, if needed, to keep beans covered.) Add carrots; simmer, covered, 30 minutes. Remove spice bag. Serves 6 to 8.

Sauerbraten

1½ cups red wine vinegar
2 medium onions, sliced
1 lemon, sliced
1 tablespoon sugar
1 tablespoon salt
¼ teaspoon ground ginger
12 whole cloves
6 bay leaves
6 whole black peppercorns
1 4-pound boned and rolled
    beef rump roast
2 tablespoons cooking oil
½ cup chopped onion
½ cup chopped carrot
¼ cup chopped celery
1 cup broken gingersnaps
Hot buttered noodles

In crock or large bowl combine first 9 ingredients and 2½ cups water; add meat. Cover; refrigerate 36 to 72 hours. Turn meat occasionally. Remove meat; wipe dry with paper toweling. Strain marinade; reserve.

In Dutch oven brown the meat on all sides in hot oil. Add reserved marinade, chopped onion, carrot, and celery. Cover; cook slowly till meat is tender, about 2 hours. Remove meat to platter; keep hot. Reserve 2 cups of the liquid in Dutch oven; add gingersnaps and ⅔ cup water. Cook and stir till thick and bubbly. Serve meat and sauce with noodles. Serves 8 to 10.

Pot Roast with Vegetable Gravy

In Dutch oven brown one 3- to 4-pound beef chuck roast in 2 tablespoons hot cooking oil; sprinkle with 1 teaspoon salt and dash pepper. Add ½ cup chopped carrot; ½ cup chopped turnip; ½ cup chopped green pepper; ½ cup chopped onion; ½ cup chopped celery; ¼ cup water; 2 tablespoons snipped parsley; and 1 clove garlic, minced. Cover and simmer till meat is tender, 1½ to 2 hours.

Remove meat to serving platter; keep hot. Skim fat from pan juices. Measure juices with vegetables; add water, if needed, to make 2 cups. Return to Dutch oven. Stir ½ cup cold water into ¼ cup all-purpose flour; stir into juices. Cook and stir till thickened and bubbly. Season to taste; serve with roast. Serves 8.

Fruit-Glazed Corned Beef

Corn your own brisket, or use commercially corned beef for this roast (shown on page 33)—

Corned Beef Brisket
Whole cloves
½ cup packed brown sugar
2 teaspoons grated orange peel
1 teaspoon grated lemon peel
½ teaspoon dry mustard
½ cup apple cider *or* apple juice
⅓ cup orange juice
2 tablespoons lemon juice

Place Corned Beef Brisket in Dutch oven and barely cover with water. Cover pan; simmer till almost tender, 3 to 4 hours. Remove from heat; cool meat in cooking liquid. Drain. Place meat in shallow roasting pan; score fat and stud with cloves. Mix sugar, peels, and mustard; pat onto meat. Combine cider, orange juice, and lemon juice; pour over meat. Bake at 350° for 1 hour; baste occasionally. Serves 12 to 15.

Corned Beef Brisket: Place one 5- to 6-pound boneless fresh beef brisket in crock, cutting meat in half or thirds, if necessary to fit. Dissolve ¼ teaspoon saltpeter in ¼ cup warm water. Add 2 tablespoons sugar; 1 tablespoon mixed pickling spice; 2 cloves garlic, minced; and 2 teaspoons paprika. Dissolve ¾ cup salt in 8 cups water; stir in saltpeter mixture. Pour over beef. Cover meat with plate; weight down to keep under brine. Refrigerate 3 weeks; turn occasionally. Drain; rinse, if desired.

Kraut and Brisket

2 pounds boneless fresh
    beef brisket
2 medium onions, sliced
1 bay leaf
1 27-ounce can sauerkraut
1 medium potato, peeled and
    shredded (1 cup)
1 teaspoon caraway seed

Trim excess fat from meat. Place fat side down in skillet; brown on both sides. Add onions, bay leaf, ½ cup water, and 1 teaspoon salt. Cover; simmer 1½ hours. Drain sauerkraut; add to meat with potato and caraway. Simmer, covered, till meat is tender, about 30 minutes longer. Remove bay leaf. Makes 6 to 8 servings.

Hearty Vegetable Soup
This flavor-rich soup is shown on page 32 —

      3 pounds beef shank cross cuts
      8 cups water
      4 teaspoons salt
      ½ teaspoon dried oregano, crushed
      ¼ teaspoon dried marjoram,
          crushed
      5 whole black peppercorns
      2 bay leaves
      1 16-ounce can tomatoes, cut up
      1 15½-ounce can red kidney beans
      2 cups frozen whole small onions
          or 3 medium onions, quartered
      1 medium turnip, peeled and diced
      1 cup sliced celery
      1 cup sliced carrot

In large saucepan or Dutch oven place beef, water, salt, oregano, marjoram, peppercorns, and bay leaves. Bring to boiling; reduce heat and simmer, covered, 2 hours. Remove beef; cut meat from bones in large cubes. Strain broth; skim off excess fat. Return broth to saucepan; add meat, undrained tomatoes, beans, onions, turnip, celery, and carrot. Simmer, covered, 1 hour. Season to taste with salt and pepper. Serves 10 to 12.

Split Pea-Vegetable Soup

      2¼ cups dry green split peas,
          rinsed (1 pound)
      1 16-ounce can tomatoes, cut up
      ½ cup chopped onion
      ½ cup chopped celery
      ¼ cup chopped carrot
      3 tablespoons snipped parsley
      2 tablespoons vinegar
      1 clove garlic, minced
      2½ teaspoons salt
      ½ teaspoon dried oregano, crushed
      6 slices bacon, crisp-cooked,
          drained, and crumbled

In large saucepan or Dutch oven combine peas, and 8 cups cold water. Add undrained tomatoes, onion, celery, carrot, parsley, vinegar, garlic, salt, and oregano. Bring to boiling; reduce heat and simmer, covered, 2 hours. Add bacon; simmer, covered, 15 minutes more. Season with salt and pepper. Serves 8 to 10.

Borscht

      3 pounds beef shank cross cuts
      8 cups water
      2 medium onions, chopped
          • • •
      2 16-ounce cans whole beets,
          shredded, *or* 2 16-ounce
          cans shoestring beets
      3 cups shredded cabbage
      1 16-ounce can lima beans,
          drained
      2 cups chopped carrots
      1 8-ounce can tomato sauce
      3 tablespoons lemon juice
      1 tablespoon sugar
      2 teaspoons salt
      ⅛ teaspoon pepper
          Dairy sour cream

In large kettle brown the meat; add water and onion. Simmer, covered, till meat is tender, about 2 hours. Remove beef; cut meat from bones. Skim fat from broth; add meat, undrained beets, and remaining ingredients *except* sour cream. Simmer, covered, till vegetables are tender, about 30 minutes. Serve hot; pass sour cream to top individual servings. Serves 12.

Sausage Supper
Kraut, apple, and sausage combo shown on page 4 —

      1 16-ounce can applesauce
          (2 cups)
      1 16-ounce can sauerkraut,
          drained and snipped (2 cups)
      ⅓ cup water
      2 tablespoons packed brown sugar
      ½ teaspoon salt
      4 small onions, quartered
      4 small potatoes, peeled and
          quartered
      1 12-ounce Polish sausage
          Snipped parsley

In 3-quart saucepan combine applesauce, sauerkraut, water, brown sugar, and salt; add onions and potatoes. Simmer, covered, 20 minutes, stirring occasionally. Add sausage; simmer, covered, about 20 minutes longer, stirring occasionally. To serve, spoon sauerkraut mixture onto serving platter; top with sausage. Sprinkle with parsley. Makes 4 servings.

Liver and Apple Skillet

1 cup chopped onion
1 medium apple, peeled, cored, and sliced (1 cup)
5 tablespoons butter *or* margarine
1 pound beef liver, thinly sliced
¼ cup all-purpose flour
1 teaspoon instant beef bouillon granules
½ teaspoon Worcestershire sauce
2 tablespoons cold water
1 tablespoon all-purpose flour
Hot cooked noodles

In skillet cook onion and apple in *2 tablespoons* of the butter till crisp-tender, 3 to 5 minutes; remove from skillet. Coat liver with mixture of ¼ cup flour, ½ teaspoon salt, and dash pepper. In same skillet brown the liver in remaining 3 tablespoons butter, 3 to 4 minutes on *each* side. Remove liver; keep warm.

To skillet add bouillon granules, Worcestershire, and 1 cup water; cook and stir till granules dissolve. Stir cold water into 1 tablespoon flour; stir into bouillon mixture. Cook and stir till thickened and bubbly. Add liver, onion, and apple; heat through. Serve over hot cooked noodles. Makes 4 servings.

MAIN DISH SEASONING GUIDE

Perk up the flavor of main dishes by using herbs and spices. Be sure that your supply of dry seasonings is fresh for best flavor. Avoid flavor loss of dry seasonings by purchasing small quantities, then storing them in airtight containers in a cool place. If you'd rather use fresh herbs, grow them from seed either in small pots or in a vegetable garden. Use the listing below as a guide for experimenting with seasonings. If herbs are dried in leaf form, crush the herb before adding; snip fresh herbs and add three times as much as when using dried herbs.

Allspice
Baked Ham
Beef Stew
Shellfish

Basil
Beef Stew
Lamb Chops
Shrimp Creole

Bay Leaf
Corned Beef
Meat Stew
Pot Roast

Chili Powder
Chicken
Meat Stew
Shellfish

Clove
Baked Ham
Meat Stew
Roast Pork

Curry Powder
Beef Stew
Poultry
Seafood

Dill
Broiled Fish
Chicken
Lamb Chops

Ginger
Chicken
Meat Stew
Pot Roast

Marjoram
Chicken
Creamed Fish
Lamb

Mint
Cold Fish
Lamb Chops
Veal Roast

Mustard
Cheese Dishes
Meat Loaf
Seafood

Nutmeg
Chicken Soup
Fish Chowder
Meat Loaf

Oregano
Beef Stew
Pizza
Seafood Salad

Paprika
Broiled Fish
Chicken
Chili

Pepper-Red
Beef Stew
Cheese Dishes
Seafood Chowder

Pepper-White
Chicken Salad
Fish
Ham Steak

Rosemary
Chicken
Hash
Lamb Stew

Saffron
Fish Chowder
Poultry
Shellfish

Sage
Pork Chops
Stuffing
Veal Roast

Thyme
Beef Stew
Fish Sauce
Fried Chicken

Notable Salads and Vegetables

In the past, the serving of salads and vegetables often was based on what the home garden had to offer. Today, freezing and canning make most fruits and vegetables plentiful throughout the year. The recipes in this section include adaptations of popular old-time salads and vegetables. Fortunately for us, they can be prepared and enjoyed any day of the year.

Confetti Pea Salad

    3½ cups water
    1 cup dry whole peas, rinsed
    ½ teaspoon salt
    3 hard-cooked eggs, chopped
    ½ cup chopped celery
    ½ cup coarsely grated carrot
    ¼ cup sweet pickle relish
    1 tablespoon chopped onion
    ½ cup mayonnaise *or* salad
        dressing
    ½ cup shredded American cheese
        (2 ounces)
    1 teaspoon salad seasoning
    1 teaspoon prepared mustard

In medium saucepan bring water and peas to boiling; boil 2 minutes. Remove from heat. Cover; let stand 1 hour. (Or, add peas to water; soak overnight.) Do not drain. Add salt; bring to boiling. Reduce heat; simmer, covered, till just tender, about 2 hours. Remove from heat; drain. Cool. Toss peas with eggs, celery, carrot, relish, and onion. Mix mayonnaise and remaining ingredients; toss with pea mixture. Cover; chill. Makes 4 servings.

Orange Waldorf Salad

Carefully combine 1½ cups diced oranges, 1 cup diced unpeeled apple, ½ cup chopped celery, and ¼ cup chopped walnuts. Combine ½ cup dairy sour cream, 2 teaspoons honey, and dash salt; fold into fruit mixture. Spoon onto lettuce-lined salad plates. Garnish with additional walnuts, if desired. Makes 4 to 6 servings.

Creamy Egg Coleslaw

    5 hard-cooked eggs
    4 cups finely shredded
        red cabbage
    2 tablespoons finely
        chopped onion
    2 tablespoons sweet pickle relish
    ½ cup mayonnaise *or* salad
        dressing
    2 teaspoons prepared mustard
    ½ teaspoon salt
    Dash pepper

Reserve 2 of the egg yolks; chop remaining eggs into medium-size pieces. Mix chopped egg, red cabbage, onion, and pickle relish. Combine mayonnaise, mustard, salt, and pepper; toss with cabbage mixture. Turn into serving bowl. Sieve reserved egg yolks atop salad. Sprinkle with paprika, if desired. Serves 4.

Garden-Fresh Tomato Aspic

    8 large tomatoes
    1 3-ounce package lemon-flavored
        gelatin
    2 tablespoons catsup
    1 tablespoon lemon juice
    2 teaspoons prepared horseradish
    1½ teaspoons Worcestershire sauce
    ¾ cup finely chopped celery
    ¼ cup finely chopped onion
    ¼ cup finely chopped green pepper

Cut off stem ends of tomatoes. Prepare tomato shells by scooping out pulp; reserve pulp. Drain tomato shells. Place reserved pulp in blender container. Cover; blend till pureed. Sieve to get 2 cups pulp with juice; combine with gelatin. Bring to boiling; stir to dissolve gelatin. Remove from heat; stir in catsup, next 3 ingredients, ½ teaspoon salt, and dash pepper. Chill till partially set. Fold in vegetables. Sprinkle insides of tomato shells with salt. Fill with gelatin mixture. Chill till firm. Serve on spinach leaves with mayonnaise, if desired. Makes 8 servings.

Cranberry Relish Mold

Chill in a star-shaped mold for holiday menus—

- 2 cups cranberries
- ½ cup sugar
- 1 3-ounce package lemon- *or* cherry-flavored gelatin
- 1 cup boiling water
- 1 8¼-ounce can crushed pineapple
- 1 cup chopped celery
- ½ cup chopped walnuts

Grind cranberries through food grinder, using coarse blade. Combine ground cranberries and sugar; set aside. Dissolve gelatin in boiling water. Drain pineapple, reserving syrup; add enough water to reserved syrup to make 1 cup. Add syrup mixture to dissolved gelatin; chill till partially set. Fold ground cranberry mixture, crushed pineapple, chopped celery, and chopped walnuts into partially set gelatin. Pour into 5-cup mold. Chill till firm. Unmold to serve. Makes 6 to 8 servings.

Strawberry-Banana Mold

Serve either as a salad or a dessert—

- 1 6-ounce package strawberry- *or* strawberry/banana-flavored gelatin
- 1 10-ounce package frozen strawberries
- 2 bananas
- ½ cup whipping cream
- ½ cup mayonnaise *or* salad dressing

Dissolve gelatin in 2 cups boiling water. Add frozen strawberries, breaking into small chunks with fork; stir till completely thawed. Stir in 1 cup cold water. Chill till partially set. Slice bananas on the bias into gelatin mixture; stir gently. Pour into 6-cup fluted mold. Chill till firm. Unmold on large platter; garnish with greens and additional banana slices, if desired. Whip cream; fold in mayonnaise. Serve with salad. Serves 8 to 10.

Strawberries and bananas share equal billing in fluted *Strawberry-Banana Mold*. To speed setting time for this shimmering mold, stir frozen strawberries directly into the hot gelatin. Serve with a fluffy whipped cream-mayonnaise dressing and bias-cut banana slices for a picture-pretty salad.

Tomato-Corn Bake

3 small tomatoes
1 cup cooked or canned corn
½ cup shredded Swiss cheese
   (2 ounces)
1 tablespoon sliced green onion

Cut tomatoes in half crosswise; remove seeds and most of pulp from center of each. (Set pulp aside to use as desired.) Sprinkle tomato shells with salt. Combine corn, cheese, and onion. Firmly pack *2 to 3 tablespoons* of the mixture into *each* tomato half. Place in shallow baking pan. Bake at 350° for 20 to 25 minutes. Serves 6.

Saucy Dilled Butternut Squash

4 cups peeled, cubed butternut
   squash (about 1½ pounds)
2 tablespoons sliced green onion
1 tablespoon butter *or* margarine
½ cup dairy sour cream
2 tablespoons milk
¼ teaspoon dried dillweed

Cook squash in boiling salted water till tender, about 10 minutes; drain well. Cook onion in butter till tender; blend in sour cream, milk, ¼ teaspoon salt, and dash pepper. Heat through, *but do not boil.* Arrange squash on serving plate; top with sour cream mixture. Sprinkle with dillweed. Makes 6 servings.

Turnip Whip

3 teaspoons instant chicken
   bouillon granules
2 pounds turnips, peeled and
   cubed (about 7 cups)
2 tablespoons chopped onion
1 tablespoon butter *or* margarine
1 tablespoon snipped parsley
½ teaspoon sugar

In large saucepan combine bouillon granules and 3 cups water; heat till granules dissolve and water is boiling. Add turnips; simmer, uncovered, till tender, about 20 minutes. Drain. In same saucepan cook onion in butter. With electric mixer, whip turnips till fluffy; mixture will not be smooth. Stir onion, parsley, and sugar into turnips. Makes 6 to 8 servings.

Corn and Rice Especiale

This casserole is pictured on page 32 —

¾ cup regular rice
½ cup chopped green pepper
3 tablespoons sliced green onion
3 tablespoons butter *or* margarine
2 17-ounce cans cream-style corn
1 17-ounce can whole kernel
   corn, drained
4 beaten eggs
½ cup milk
1 teaspoon salt
1 cup coarsely crushed round
   cheese crackers (18 crackers)
Paprika

Cook rice according to package directions. Cook green pepper and onion in butter till tender but not brown; stir into rice with cream-style corn, whole kernel corn, eggs, milk, and salt. Turn into 12x7½x2-inch baking dish. Bake, covered, at 375° till knife inserted in center comes out clean, 40 to 45 minutes. Sprinkle cracker crumbs and paprika around edge. Bake, uncovered, about 5 minutes longer. Makes 10 to 12 servings.

Cheesy Brussels Sprouts Bake

2 10-ounce packages frozen
   Brussels sprouts
2 beaten eggs
1 10¾-ounce can condensed
   cream of mushroom soup
1½ cups soft bread crumbs
   (2 slices bread)
½ cup shredded sharp American
   cheese (2 ounces)
2 tablespoons chopped onion
   Dash pepper
1 tablespoon butter *or*
   margarine, melted

Cook Brussels sprouts according to package directions; drain. Cut sprouts into quarters. Combine eggs, soup, ½ cup of the soft bread crumbs, cheese, onion, and pepper; stir in Brussels sprouts. Turn mixture into 1½-quart casserole. Toss remaining 1 cup soft bread crumbs with melted butter or margarine; sprinkle crumbs over casserole. Bake at 350° for 50 to 55 minutes. Makes 6 to 8 servings.

Hot Potato Salad

4 medium potatoes (1½ pounds)
6 slices bacon
2 tablespoons chopped onion
2 tablespoons cornstarch
½ teaspoon salt
⅔ cup *sweetened condensed* milk
½ cup vinegar

Cook potatoes in boiling salted water till tender, 35 to 40 minutes; drain. Peel, thinly slice, and season with a little salt and pepper; keep warm. Cook bacon till crisp; drain, reserving 2 tablespoons drippings. Cook onion in reserved drippings till tender but not brown; stir in cornstarch and ½ teaspoon salt. Combine sweetened condensed milk and ⅔ cup water; add to onion mixture. Cook and stir till thickened and bubbly. Blend in vinegar. Crumble bacon; add to potatoes. Pour hot dressing over warm potatoes. Garnish with parsley, if desired. Serve warm. Makes 6 servings.

Double-Decker Potatoes

This novel potato dish is shown on page 4 —

2 small baking potatoes
2 tablespoons butter *or* margarine, melted
3 medium potatoes, peeled and cubed (1 pound)
¼ cup chopped green onion
1 tablespoon butter *or* margarine
½ cup dairy sour cream
½ teaspoon salt
⅓ cup shredded sharp American cheese (1½ ounces)

Scrub baking potatoes; do not peel. Cut each baking potato lengthwise into 3 slices. Place, cut side up, in 12x7½x2-inch baking dish. Brush with melted butter. Sprinkle with a little salt and pepper; cover. Bake at 350° till potatoes are tender, 30 to 35 minutes.

Cook cubed potatoes in boiling water till tender. Drain; mash. Cook onion in 1 tablespoon butter; stir into mashed potatoes with sour cream, salt, and dash pepper. Spoon about ⅓ *cup* of the potato mixture atop each baked potato slice. Bake, uncovered, at 350° for 10 minutes. Top with cheese; return to oven till cheese melts, about 5 minutes. Serves 6.

Springtime Potatoes

1½ pounds small new potatoes
½ cup dairy sour cream
⅓ cup chopped seeded cucumber
2 tablespoons chopped green onion
2 tablespoons chopped green pepper
2 tablespoons sliced radishes
1 tablespoon milk

Scrub potatoes; cook in boiling salted water till tender, 15 to 25 minutes. Drain. Stir together sour cream, vegetables, milk, ½ teaspoon salt, and dash pepper. Stir over low heat till hot; *do not boil.* Pour over hot potatoes. Serves 4.

Braised Lettuce

2 tablespoons finely chopped onion
2 tablespoons finely chopped carrot
1 tablespoon butter *or* margarine
½ cup chicken broth
2 teaspoons sugar
1 medium head lettuce, shredded (6 cups)
1 5-ounce can water chestnuts, drained and sliced
Snipped parsley

In saucepan cook onion and carrot in butter till tender. Stir in chicken broth, sugar, and ½ teaspoon salt. Add lettuce and water chestnuts. Cover; simmer over low heat 5 to 8 minutes. Drain; transfer to serving dish. Sprinkle with parsley. Top with toasted slivered almonds, if desired, Makes 6 servings.

Bean Pot-Baked Lentils

Rinse 1 cup dry lentils; drain. In saucepan combine lentils, 2½ cups water, ½ cup chopped onion, and 1 teaspoon salt. Bring to boiling; reduce heat. Simmer, covered, 45 minutes. Dice 2 slices bacon; stir into lentils with 2 tablespoons packed brown sugar, 2 tablespoons catsup, 2 tablespoons molasses, and ½ teaspoon dry mustard. Turn into 1-quart bean pot or casserole. Bake, uncovered, at 350° for 1¼ hours; stir occasionally. Makes 4 to 6 servings.

Homespun Baked Goods

Here is your guide to making home-baked specialties similar to those every homemaker prepared as a part of her daily routine in pioneer days. The collection on the next few pages includes recipes for pies, cookies, cakes, yeast breads, sweet rolls, quick breads, and coffee cakes—all featuring a built-in aroma your family will find hard to resist.

Gooseberry Pie

      3 cups gooseberries, washed and
         stemmed
  1½ cups sugar
      3 tablespoons quick-cooking
         tapioca
      ¼ teaspoon salt
         Pastry for 2-crust 9-inch pie
      2 tablespoons butter or margarine

Crush ½ cup of the berries. In saucepan combine crushed berries, sugar, tapioca, and salt; cook and stir till thickened and bubbly. Remove from heat; stir in rest of berries. Line 9-inch pie plate with pastry. Pour in filling; dot with butter. Adjust top crust; seal and flute edges. Cut slits for escape of steam. Bake at 400° till browned, 30 to 40 minutes.

Lemon-Pear Pie

      1 beaten egg
      1 cup sugar
      1 teaspoon grated lemon peel
      ¼ cup lemon juice
      1 tablespoon butter or margarine
      1 29-ounce can pear halves
         Pastry for 2-crust 9-inch pie

In saucepan combine egg, sugar, peel, lemon juice, and butter. Cook and stir over low heat till thickened and bubbly; remove from heat. Drain and dice pears. Line 9-inch pie plate with pastry; fill with pears. Pour lemon mixture over pears. Adjust top crust; seal and flute edges. Cut slits for escape of steam. Bake at 400° till golden brown, about 35 minutes.

Rhubarb and Cherry Pie

      1 pound rhubarb, cut in ½-inch
         slices (about 4 cups)
      1 16-ounce can pitted tart red
         cherries, drained (2 cups)
  1½ cups sugar
      ¼ cup quick-cooking tapioca
      5 drops red food coloring
         Pastry for 9-inch
            lattice-top pie

Combine fruits, sugar, tapioca, and food coloring; let stand 15 minutes. Line 9-inch pie plate with pastry; pour in filling. Adjust lattice top; seal and flute edges. Bake at 400° for 40 to 50 minutes; cover pastry edges with foil to avoid overbrowning, if needed.

Deep-Dish Apple Pie

This all-American dessert is shown on page 4—

    12 medium tart apples
      1 cup sugar
      3 tablespoons all-purpose flour
      ½ teaspoon ground cinnamon
      ¼ teaspoon ground nutmeg
      3 tablespoons butter or margarine
      1 cup all-purpose flour
      ⅓ cup shortening
         Cold milk
         Sugar
         Light cream

Peel, core, and thinly slice apples (11 cups); place in large bowl. Mix 1 cup sugar, 3 tablespoons flour, cinnamon, nutmeg, and ¼ teaspoon salt; sprinkle over apples. Mix well. Turn into 12x7½x2-inch baking dish; dot with butter. Stir 1 cup flour with ⅛ teaspoon salt; cut in shortening till crumbly. Gradually add 2 to 3 tablespoons milk; toss with fork to just dampen. Form into a ball. On lightly floured surface roll to 13x8½-inch rectangle. Place over apples; flute edges. Brush with milk; cut slits for escape of steam. Sprinkle with sugar. Bake at 400° for 40 to 45 minutes. Serve warm with cream. Makes 8 servings.

Rhubarb and cherries provide the winning combination in this flavor-packed fruit pie. Made with brightly colored fresh rhubarb and canned tart red cherries, *Rhubarb and Cherry Pie* is a delight for pie fans. For added enjoyment, serve the pie warm and top with a big scoop of vanilla ice cream.

Banana Cream Pie

    2 eggs, separated
    ⅓ cup sugar
    3 tablespoons cornstarch
 1½ cups milk
    2 tablespoons butter *or* margarine
    2 teaspoons vanilla
    ¼ cup sugar
    1 *baked* 9-inch pastry shell,
      cooled
    2 bananas, sliced (1½ cups)

Beat egg yolks. Mix ⅓ cup sugar, cornstarch, and ¼ teaspoon salt; stir in milk, then yolks. Cook and stir over medium heat until mixture bubbles; cook and stir 2 minutes longer. Remove from heat. Stir in butter and vanilla. Cool. Beat whites till soft peaks form; slowly add ¼ cup sugar. Beat till stiff peaks form. Fold into yolk mixture. Alternate layers of banana and filling in pastry shell. Cover; chill.

Chocolate-Topped Custard Pie

So good, you'll want to serve this to friends —

    3 slightly beaten eggs
    ½ cup sugar
    ¼ teaspoon salt
    ¼ teaspoon ground nutmeg
    2 cups scalded milk
    1 *unbaked* 8-inch pastry shell
    ½ cup milk chocolate pieces
    4 teaspoons milk
    Milk

Combine eggs, sugar, salt, and nutmeg. Stir in hot milk; mix well. Pour into unbaked pastry shell. Bake at 425° till knife inserted just off-center comes out clean, about 25 minutes. Cool. Melt chocolate with 4 teaspoons milk over low heat, stirring constantly. Remove from heat; stir in additional milk, a few drops at a time, till of spreading consistency. Quickly spread over pie; chill.

Date-Filled Sugar Cookies

These old-fashioned cookies are shown on page 4 —

    Date Filling
  1 cup shortening
  ½ cup granulated sugar
  ½ cup packed brown sugar
  1 egg
  ¼ cup milk
  1 teaspoon vanilla
  3 cups all-purpose flour
  ½ teaspoon baking soda

Prepare Date Filling; set aside. Cream shortening with sugars. Add egg, milk, and vanilla; beat well. Stir flour with soda and ½ teaspoon salt; add to creamed mixture. Mix well. Cover; chill 1 hour. Halve dough. On lightly floured surface roll *each* half to ⅛-inch thickness; cut into 2-inch rounds with cookie cutter. Place *half* of the rounds on ungreased cookie sheet; top *each* with *about* ½ *teaspoon* of the filling. Cover with plain rounds; seal edges with floured tip of teaspoon. Bake at 375° for 6 to 8 minutes. Makes 48.

Date Filling: Bring ⅔ cup snipped pitted dates, 3 tablespoons water, 2 tablespoons granulated sugar, and dash salt to boiling; reduce heat. Cover; simmer 2 to 3 minutes. Remove from heat; stir in ¼ cup chopped walnuts (optional) and 1½ teaspoons lemon juice.

Currant Pound Cake

  1 cup dried currants
  ¼ cup brandy
  2 cups butter *or* margarine,
    softened (1 pound)
2¼ cups sugar
  8 eggs (room temperature)
  4 cups all-purpose flour
  ½ teaspoon ground nutmeg

In jar combine currants and brandy; cover tightly. Soak at room temperature several hours or overnight. Drain well. Cream butter. Slowly add sugar; cream till fluffy. Add eggs one at a time, beating well after each (about 10 minutes total beating for eggs). Stir flour with nutmeg; add to creamed mixture. Stir well. Fold in currants. Grease *bottom only* of two 9x5x3-inch loaf pans. Turn batter into pans. Bake at 325° for 60 to 65 minutes. Makes 2.

Refrigerator Fruit Cookies

  1 cup butter *or* margarine,
    softened
  1 cup granulated sugar
  1 cup packed brown sugar
  2 eggs
  1 teaspoon vanilla
2½ cups all-purpose flour
  1 teaspoon baking soda
  ½ teaspoon ground cinnamon
  1 cup finely chopped nuts
  1 cup finely snipped pitted dates
  ½ cup finely chopped red
    candied cherries

Cream butter with sugars. Add eggs and vanilla; beat well. Stir flour with soda, cinnamon, and ½ teaspoon salt; stir into creamed mixture. Stir in nuts and fruits. Form into two 10-inch rolls. Wrap in waxed paper or clear plastic wrap; chill well. Slice ¼ inch thick; arrange 2 inches apart on ungreased cookie sheet. Bake at 375° for 8 to 10 minutes. Makes about 78 cookies.

Cherry-Topped Sponge Cake

  ¾ cup egg yolks (8)
  ⅔ cup sugar
  1 teaspoon grated orange peel
  ½ cup orange juice
  1 cup sifted cake flour
  1 cup egg whites (8)
  1 teaspoon cream of tartar
  ⅔ cup sugar
1½ cups whipping cream
  2 tablespoons sugar
  1 pound fresh dark sweet cherries,
    pitted and quartered

Beat yolks till thick and lemon-colored; slowly add ⅔ cup sugar. Beat till thick. Mix peel and juice; beat into yolks alternately with flour. Beat whites with cream of tartar and ½ teaspoon salt till soft peaks form. Slowly add ⅔ cup sugar, beating till stiff peaks form. Fold into yolk mixture. Turn into *ungreased* 10-inch tube pan; bake at 325° for 1 hour. Invert pan; cool. Remove from pan; split cake into 3 layers. Whip cream with 2 tablespoons sugar. Assemble cake, spooning cream and cherries between layers and on top.

Oatmeal Spice Cake

    1 cup quick-cooking rolled oats
    1 cup granulated sugar
    1 cup packed brown sugar
    ½ cup shortening
    2 eggs
    1⅓ cups all-purpose flour
    2½ teaspoons baking powder
    1 teaspoon ground cinnamon
    ¾ teaspoon ground nutmeg
    ¾ teaspoon ground ginger
    Broiled Frosting

Pour 1¼ cups boiling water over oats; let stand 20 minutes. Cream sugars with shortening till fluffy. Add eggs one at a time, beating well after each. Add oat mixture; mix well. Stir flour with baking powder, spices, and ½ teaspoon salt; stir into oat batter. Mix well. Turn into greased and floured 13x9x2-inch baking pan. Bake at 350° for 35 to 40 minutes. Cool slightly; spread Broiled Frosting over cake. Broil 4 to 5 inches from heat till bubbly, about 1 minute. Serve warm or cool.

Broiled Frosting: Combine ½ cup packed brown sugar, 6 tablespoons butter, ¼ cup milk, and 2 tablespoons light corn syrup. Cook and stir over medium heat till mixture boils; reduce heat. Simmer till thick, 2 to 3 minutes; stir constantly. Remove from heat; stir in ½ cup shredded coconut and ½ cup chopped nuts.

Lemon Cake with Pudding Sauce

This homey dessert is pictured on page 50—

Cream 1 cup sugar with ¾ cup shortening till fluffy. Add 3 eggs, one at a time, beating well after each. Stir in ½ teaspoon lemon extract. Stir 2 cups all-purpose flour with 1½ teaspoons baking powder and ¼ teaspoon salt. Add to creamed mixture alternately with ½ cup milk, beating well after each addition. Reserve ½ *cup* of the batter for sauce. Turn remaining batter into greased 9x9x2-inch baking pan. Bake at 375° for 25 to 30 minutes.

For pudding sauce, combine 2 cups warm water, ¾ cup sugar, reserved batter, ½ teaspoon lemon extract, and ¼ teaspoon vanilla; mix well. Cook and stir till thickened and bubbly; remove from heat. Stir in 2 tablespoons butter. Serve over warm cake. Serves 9.

Maple-Frosted Golden Cake

    2 cups all-purpose flour
    1¼ cups sugar
    2½ teaspoons baking powder
    1 teaspoon salt
    1 cup milk
    ½ cup shortening
    2 eggs
    1 teaspoon vanilla
    Maple Frosting

In mixing bowl stir together flour, sugar, baking powder, and salt. Add ¾ *cup* of the milk and shortening. Beat 2 minutes at medium speed of electric mixer. Add remaining ¼ cup milk, eggs, and vanilla; beat 2 minutes longer. Pour batter into 2 greased and floured 8x1½-inch round baking pans. Bake at 350° for 35 to 40 minutes. Cool 5 minutes; remove cake from pans. Cool thoroughly. Fill and frost cake with Maple Frosting.

Maple Frosting: In saucepan cook 1¼ cups maple-flavored syrup to soft-ball stage (238°). Gradually add hot syrup to 2 stiffly beaten egg whites, beating constantly with electric mixer. Blend in ¼ cup sifted powdered sugar.

Black Walnut Cake

Cream ¾ cup granulated sugar, ½ cup softened butter *or* margarine, and ¼ cup packed brown sugar. Add 2 eggs, one at a time; beat well after each. Mix 1 teaspoon grated orange peel, ½ cup orange juice, ¼ cup molasses, and ½ teaspoon vanilla. Stir 2 cups all-purpose flour with 1 tablespoon baking powder, ½ teaspoon ground nutmeg, ¼ teaspoon salt, ¼ teaspoon ground cinnamon, and dash ground cloves. Add to creamed mixture alternately with juice mixture; mix well after each addition. Stir in 1 cup chopped black walnuts and ½ cup raisins. Pour into greased and floured 9x9x2-inch baking pan. Bake at 350° for 40 to 45 minutes. Cool. Frost with Orange Frosting.

Orange Frosting: Cream 3 tablespoons softened butter. Slowly add 1¼ cups sifted powdered sugar; blend well. Beat in 2 tablespoons orange juice and 1 teaspoon vanilla. Slowly blend in another 1¼ cups sifted powdered sugar. Stir in enough additional orange juice to make frosting of spreading consistency.

Baking at home is fun, especially when the fruits of your labor are as tempting as these breads and desserts. Shown are *Pan Rolls, Sesame Braid,* and *Light Bread*—all made from one dough; *Cheese Bread; Dill-Cottage Cheese Bread,* and *Lemon Cake with Pudding Sauce* (see recipe, page 49).

Cheese Bread

In large mixing bowl stir 1¾ cups all-purpose flour with 2 packages active dry yeast. In saucepan heat 1¼ cups water, ¼ cup sugar, and 1½ teaspoons salt just till warm (115-120°), stirring constantly. Add to dry mixture in bowl; add 2 cups shredded sharp American cheese (8 ounces) and 1 egg. Beat at low speed of electric mixer ½ minute, scraping bowl. Beat 3 minutes at high speed. By hand, stir in 1¾ to 2¼ cups all-purpose flour to make a moderately stiff dough.

Knead on floured surface till smooth (3 to 5 minutes). Place in greased bowl; turn once to grease surface. Cover; let rise till double (1¼ to 1½ hours). Punch down; halve dough. Cover; let rest 10 minutes. Shape into 2 loaves; place in 2 greased 8½x4½x2½-inch loaf pans. Cover; let rise till almost double (about 45 minutes). Bake at 350° for 40 to 45 minutes. Remove from pans; cool. Makes 2 loaves.

Dill-Cottage Cheese Bread

In large mixing bowl mix 1 cup all-purpose flour, 1 package active dry yeast, 1 tablespoon finely chopped onion, 2 teaspoons dried dill-seed, and ¼ teaspoon baking soda. Heat 1 cup cream-style cottage cheese, ¼ cup water, ¼ cup shortening, 2 tablespoons sugar, and 1 teaspoon salt just till warm (115-120°); stir constantly. Add to dry mixture; add 1 egg. Beat at low speed of electric mixer ½ minute, scraping bowl. Beat 3 minutes at high speed.

By hand, stir in 1¼ to 1½ cups all-purpose flour to make a soft dough. Knead till smooth (about 5 minutes). Place in greased bowl; turn once. Cover; let rise till double (about 1 hour). Punch down; cover. Let rest 10 minutes. Shape into loaf; place in greased 9x5x3-inch loaf pan. Cover; let rise till almost double (30 to 45 minutes). Bake at 350° for 40 minutes. Remove from pan. Brush with melted butter; top with dried dillseed. Makes 1 loaf.

Light Bread

6 to 6½ cups all-purpose flour
2 packages active dry yeast
1 cup milk
½ cup sugar
½ cup shortening
2 eggs

In large mixing bowl mix *3½ cups* of the flour and yeast. Heat milk, sugar, shortening, 1 cup water, and 2 teaspoons salt just till warm (115-120°), stirring constantly. Add to dry mixture; add eggs. Beat at low speed of electric mixer ½ minute; scrape bowl. Beat 3 minutes at high speed. By hand, stir in enough of the remaining flour to make a soft dough. Knead on floured surface till smooth (8 to 10 minutes). Place in greased bowl; turn once. Cover; let rise till double (about 1¼ hours). Punch down; cover. Let rest 10 minutes.

Divide into 2 or 3 pieces; shape into loaves. Place in 2 greased 9x5x3-inch loaf pans *or* 3 greased 8½x4½x2½-inch loaf pans. Cover; let rise till double (45 to 60 minutes). Bake at 400° for 25 minutes. Makes 2 or 3 loaves.

Pan Rolls: Prepare Light Bread dough, *except* after first rising, shape into 36 rolls. Place in 2 greased 13x9x2-inch baking pans. Cover; let rise till double (45 to 60 minutes). Bake at 400° for 15 to 20 minutes. Makes 36 rolls.

Sesame Braid: Prepare Light Bread dough, *except* after first rising, divide into 6 pieces; roll to 15-inch ropes. Using 3 ropes for *each*, shape into 2 braids on greased baking sheets. Cover; let rise till double. Brush with unbeaten egg white; sprinkle with sesame seed. Bake at 375° for 20 to 25 minutes. Makes 2.

Lime Bread

Stir together 3 cups all-purpose flour, ¾ cup sugar, 1 tablespoon baking powder, 1 teaspoon salt, and ¼ teaspoon baking soda. Combine 1½ cups milk, 1 beaten egg, ¼ cup cooking oil, 2 teaspoons grated lime peel, and ¼ cup lime juice. Add to dry mixture; stir just till moistened. Turn into greased 9x5x3-inch loaf pan. Bake at 350° for 1 hour. Cool 10 minutes; remove from pan. Mix 2 tablespoons sugar and 1 tablespoon lime juice; spoon atop loaf. Cool completely. Wrap; store overnight. Makes 1.

Sourdough Rye Buns

Caraway seed tops these buns shown on page 67 —

To make Sourdough Starter: In bowl soften 1 package active dry yeast in ½ cup *warm* water (110°). Stir in 2½ cups all-purpose flour, 2 cups *warm* water, and 1 tablespoon honey. Beat till smooth. Cover with cheesecloth. Let stand at room temperature till bubbly, 5 to 10 days; stir 2 or 3 times a day. (Fermentation time depends on room temperature; a warmer room will hasten the process.) Store Starter covered, in refrigerator. To use, bring desired amount of Starter to room temperature.

3¾ cups warm water (110°)
1 cup Sourdough Starter
4½ cups whole wheat flour
4 cups rye flour
½ cup cooking oil
1 tablespoon salt
¼ cup all-purpose flour
1 beaten egg white
Caraway seed *or* coarse salt

To make buns: In large mixing bowl combine warm water and Sourdough Starter. Stir in whole wheat flour; beat well. Cover mixture and let stand at room temperature for several hours, or refrigerate overnight. Add rye flour, cooking oil, and 1 tablespoon salt; mix thoroughly. Dough will be slightly sticky.

Turn out onto lightly floured surface. Knead about 5 minutes, adding enough of the ¼ cup all-purpose flour to make a soft dough. Shape into ball. Place in greased bowl, turning once to grease surface. Cover and let rise in warm place till double. Punch down; divide dough into 3 portions. Cover; let rest 5 minutes.

Divide *each* portion into 8 balls. Turn *each* ball in hands, folding edges under to make a smooth ball. Press ball flat between hands. Place on greased baking sheet, pressing each to a 3½-inch circle. Brush with egg white; sprinkle with caraway seed or coarse salt. Cover; let rise in warm place till double. Bake at 375° for 35 to 30 minutes. Makes 2 dozen.

To keep Starter going: After using some Starter, stir ¾ cup water, ¾ cup all-purpose flour, and 1 teaspoon sugar into remaining Starter. Let stand till bubbly, about 1 day. Cover; refrigerate. If not used frequently, stir in 1 teaspoon sugar every 10 days.

Blueberry Coffee Cake

2 cups all-purpose flour
½ cup granulated sugar
1 tablespoon baking powder
½ teaspoon salt
½ teaspoon ground ginger
¼ teaspoon baking soda
½ cup shortening
2 beaten eggs
½ cup buttermilk *or* sour milk
2 cups fresh or frozen
    blueberries
Streusel Topping

Stir together first 6 ingredients; cut in shortening till crumbly. Combine eggs and buttermilk; add to crumbly mixture. Beat well. Spread batter in greased 13x9x2-inch baking pan. Top with berries; sprinkle with Streusel Topping. Bake at 350° for 30 to 35 minutes. Serve warm or cool. Makes 1 coffee cake.

Streusel Topping: Combine ½ cup packed brown sugar, ¼ cup all-purpose flour, and ¼ teaspoon ground ginger. Cut in 2 tablespoons butter *or* margarine till mixture is crumbly.

Walnut-Filled Coffee Cake

¾ cup sugar
½ cup shortening
2 eggs
1½ cups all-purpose flour
2 teaspoons baking powder
1 teaspoon ground ginger
⅔ cup milk
    Nut Filling

Cream sugar and shortening. Add eggs one at a time; beat well after each. Stir flour with baking powder, ginger, and ¾ teaspoon salt. Add to creamed mixture alternately with milk; beat well after each addition. Spoon *half* of the batter into greased and floured 6½-cup ring mold. Sprinkle with Nut Filling; top with remaining batter. Bake at 350° about 35 minutes. Cool in pan 5 minutes; unmold. Sprinkle lightly with sifted powdered sugar, if desired. Serve warm. Makes 1 coffee cake.

Nut Filling: Mix ½ cup chopped walnuts, ¼ cup finely chopped candied orange peel, 2 tablespoons all-purpose flour, 1 tablespoon sugar, and 1 tablespoon softened butter.

Basic Sweet Dough

In large mixing bowl mix 2½ cups all-purpose flour and 1 package active dry yeast. Heat 2¼ cups milk, ⅓ cup sugar, ¼ cup shortening, and 2 teaspoons salt just till warm (115-120°), stirring constantly. Add to dry mixture. Beat at low speed of electric mixer ½ minute scraping bowl. Beat 3 minutes at high speed. By hand, stir in 3¼ to 3¾ cups all-purpose flour to make a moderately stiff dough. Knead on floured surface till smooth (8 to 10 minutes). Place in greased bowl; turn once. Cover; let rise till double (about 1¼ hours). Halve dough. Use *half* to prepare Swedish Tea Wreath and remaining for Cinnamon Whirl.

Swedish Tea Wreath

A colorful holiday bread shown on page 2 —

½ recipe Basic Sweet Dough
¼ cup butter *or* margarine, melted
¾ cup chopped mixed candied
    fruits and peels
    Confectioners' Icing
    (see recipe, page 22)

Roll dough to rectangle ½ inch thick. Brush with butter; sprinkle with fruits and peels. Roll up jelly-roll fashion, starting at long side. Shape into ring; seal ends together. Place on greased baking sheet. With scissors, snip ⅔ of the way through ring at 1-inch intervals; turn each section on its side. Cover; let rise till almost double. Bake at 350° for 35 minutes. Drizzle warm bread with icing; top with blanched whole almonds and candied cherries, if desired. Makes 1.

Cinnamon Whirl

This scrumptious loaf is pictured on page 2 —

Roll ½ recipe Basic Sweet Dough to 15x7-inch rectangle. Mix ¼ cup sugar and 1½ teaspoons ground cinnamon; sprinkle over dough. Sprinkle with 1½ teaspoons water. Roll into loaf, starting at short side. Place in greased and floured 9x5x3-inch loaf pan. Cover; let rise till double (45 to 60 minutes). Bake at 375° for 30 minutes. While warm, drizzle with Confectioners' Icing (see recipe, page 22). Makes 1 loaf.

Cinnamon Rolls

Glazed sweet rolls pictured on page 32 —

2¼ to 2½ cups all-purpose flour
1 package active dry yeast
¾ cup milk
¼ cup sugar
¼ cup shortening
1 egg
2 tablespoons butter *or* margarine
¼ cup chopped pecans
2 tablespoons sugar
1 teaspoon ground cinnamon
Confectioners' Icing (see
recipe, page 22)

In large mixing bowl mix *1 cup* of the flour and yeast. Heat milk, ¼ cup sugar, shortening, and 1 teaspoon salt just till warm (115-120°), stirring constantly. Add to dry mixture; add egg. Beat at low speed of electric mixer ½ minute, scraping bowl. Beat 3 minutes at high speed. By hand, stir in enough of the remaining flour to make a soft dough.

Knead on floured surface (3 to 5 minutes). Place in greased bowl; turn. Cover; let rise till double (1 to 1¼ hours). Punch down; cover. Let rest 10 minutes. Roll to 12x8-inch rectangle. Melt butter; brush over dough.

Mix nuts, 2 tablespoons sugar, and cinnamon; sprinkle over dough. Roll up jelly-roll fashion, starting at long side. Cut into twelve 1-inch rolls. Place in greased 9x9x2-inch baking pan. Cover; let rise till almost double (30 to 45 minutes). Bake at 375° for 25 to 30 minutes. Top with Icing while warm. Makes 12.

Honey-Nut Muffins

1½ cups all-purpose flour
2 teaspoons baking flour
1 beaten egg
½ cup chopped nuts
½ cup honey
⅓ cup milk
¼ cup cooking oil

Stir flour with baking powder and ½ teaspoon salt; make well in center. Combine egg, nuts, honey, milk, and oil; add all at once to dry mixture. Stir just till moistened. Fill greased 2¾-inch muffin pans ⅔ full. Bake at 375° for 15 to 18 minutes. Makes 10 muffins.

Bubble Wreath

Bake these rolls in a tube pan, as shown on page 2 —

In large mixing bowl mix 2 cups all-purpose flour and 1 package active dry yeast. Heat 1¼ cups milk, ¼ cup granulated sugar, ¼ cup shortening, and 1 teaspoon salt just till warm (115-120°), stirring constantly. Add to dry mixture; add 1 egg. Beat at low speed of electric mixer ½ minute, scraping bowl. Beat 3 minutes at high speed. By hand, stir in 1½ to 1¾ cups all-purpose flour to make a soft dough. Knead on floured surface till smooth. Place in greased bowl; turn once to grease surface. Cover; let rise till double (about 2 hours).

Melt 2 tablespoons butter; stir in ½ cup packed brown sugar and 2 tablespoons light corn syrup. Spread on bottom of greased 10-inch tube pan. Halve 16 red candied cherries; arrange, cut side up, with a few blanched slivered almonds atop sugar mixture.

Melt about ¼ cup butter. Shape dough into 48 small balls; roll in butter, then in a mixture of ½ cup granulated sugar and 1 teaspoon ground cinnamon. Layer in pan. Cover; let rise till double. Bake at 400° for 35 minutes. Loosen; turn out quickly. Makes 1 coffee cake.

Sugar Plum Loaf

This classic holiday treat is pictured on page 2 —

In large mixing bowl mix 2 cups all-purpose flour and 2 packages active dry yeast. Heat 1 cup milk, ¼ cup sugar, ¼ cup shortening, and 1½ teaspoons salt just till warm (115-120°), stirring constantly. Add to dry mixture; add 2 eggs. Beat at low speed of electric mixer ½ minute. Beat 3 minutes at high speed.

By hand, stir in 2 cups all-purpose flour to make a moderately soft dough. Stir in 1 cup chopped walnuts, ¾ cup raisins, ¼ cup chopped red candied cherries, ¼ cup chopped candied citron, 1 tablespoon chopped candied orange peel, and 1 tablespoon ground cardamom; mix well. Knead on floured surface till smooth. Place in greased bowl; turn once. Cover; let rise till double (about 2 hours). Divide in half. Cover; let rest 10 minutes. Shape into 2 round loaves; place on 2 greased baking sheets. Cover; let rise till double. Bake at 350° for 1 hour. Makes 2 loaves.

Memorable Desserts and Sweets

Sweet endings from bygone days need not be just a hazy memory. Now, you can prepare many of the desserts and between-mealtime sweets that, during childhood, made "cleaning your plate" so rewarding. Look through this section for ice cream beverages, fruit desserts, puddings, crunchy snacks, and creamy candies — all similar to those enjoyed in the past.

Minted Lime Soda

> 6 tablespoons crème de menthe
>   syrup
> 6 tablespoons lime juice
> 1 quart vanilla ice cream
> 1 28-ounce bottle lemon-lime
>   carbonated beverage, chilled
> Mint sprigs

To *each* of 6 chilled 12-ounce glasses, add *1 tablespoon* of the crème de menthe syrup and *1 tablespoon* of the lime juice. To each glass add a *small amount* of the ice cream and ½ *cup* of the carbonated beverage. Stir to muddle. Place additional scoops of ice cream in glasses; fill with remaining carbonated beverage. Garnish with mint sprigs. Makes 6 servings.

Pineapple-Orange Cooler

> Orange sherbet
> 3 cups unsweetened pineapple
>   juice, chilled
> 1 cup orange juice, chilled
> ½ teaspoon aromatic bitters
> 2 12-ounce bottles lemon-lime
>   carbonated beverage, chilled
> Orange slices, halved

In *each* of 6 chilled glasses, place *1 small scoop* of the sherbet. Combine pineapple juice, orange juice, and bitters. To each glass add a *small amount* of the juice mixture; stir to muddle. Divide remaining juice mixture among glasses. Add another scoop of sherbet to each glass; fill with carbonated beverage. Garnish with orange slices. Makes 6 servings.

Petits Fours

> 1½ cups sugar
> ¾ cup shortening
> 1½ teaspoons vanilla
> 2 cups all-purpose flour
> 1 tablespoon baking powder
> 1 cup milk
> 5 stiffly beaten egg whites
> Petits Fours Icing
> Ornamental Frosting

Cream sugar, shortening, and vanilla. Stir flour with baking powder and 1 teaspoon salt. Add to creamed mixture alternately with milk; beat after each addition. Fold in whites. Spread in greased and floured 13x9x2-inch baking pan. Bake at 350° about 30 minutes. Cool 10 minutes; remove from pan. Cool thoroughly.

Cut cake in 1½-inch squares. Place on rack over baking sheet; spoon Petits Fours Icing over cakes. Let dry; add second coat. Decorate with flowers made with Ornamental Frosting.

Petits Fours Icing: In covered 2-quart saucepan bring 3 cups granulated sugar, 1½ cups hot water, and ¼ teaspoon cream of tartar to boiling. Uncover; cook to thin syrup (226°). Cool *at room temperature* to lukewarm (110°). Blend in 1 teaspoon vanilla and enough sifted powdered sugar (about 2½ cups) to make pourable. Tint with food coloring, if desired.

Ornamental Frosting: With electric mixer blend 1 cup shortening with 1 teaspoon vanilla. Slowly add 4 cups sifted powdered sugar; beat till combined. Stir in 1½ tablespoons milk. Make trial flower with pastry tube. If frosting is too stiff, add a few more drops milk. Tint to desired color. Make flowers; place on cookie sheet. Chill 1 hour; place on cakes.

Sparkling ice cream drinks are a welcome refreshment for all ages during warm summer days. Frosty and fruity, *Minted Lime Soda* and *Pineapple-Orange Cooler* are modern-day versions of the ever-popular ice cream soda. Complete the light snack with colorful and decorative *Petits Fours*.

Steamed Blackberry Pudding

    1 cup sugar
    ½ cup butter *or* margarine
    2 eggs
    ½ teaspoon vanilla
    2 cups all-purpose flour
    1 tablespoon baking powder
    ½ teaspoon salt
    ½ teaspoon ground cinnamon
    ¾ cup milk
    2 tablespoons lemon juice
    1 16-ounce can blackberries
    Blackberry Sauce

Cream sugar and butter; add eggs and vanilla. Mix well. Stir flour with baking powder, salt, and cinnamon. Add to creamed mixture alternately with milk; beat smooth after each addition. Stir in lemon juice. Drain berries; reserve syrup for sauce. Gently fold berries into batter. Pour into greased and floured 5½-cup mold. Cover with foil; tie with string. Place on rack in deep kettle; add boiling water to kettle, 1 inch deep. Cover; steam 2 hours, adding boiling water as needed. Cool 20 minutes; unmold. Slice; serve warm with Blackberry Sauce. Makes 8 servings.

Blackberry Sauce: Add enough water to reserved blackberry syrup to make 1½ cups. Mix ¼ cup sugar and 2 tablespoons cornstarch. Gradually stir in syrup mixture. Cook and stir over medium heat till thickened and bubbly; stir in 1 tablespoon lemon juice. Makes 1⅔ cups.

Baked Rich Rice Pudding

In heavy 2-quart saucepan bring 2 cups milk, ½ cup regular rice, and ½ cup raisins to boiling; reduce heat. Cover; cook over very low heat till rice is tender, about 15 minutes. Remove from heat; stir in ¼ cup butter *or* margarine till melted. In bowl combine 2 cups milk, 3 beaten eggs, ⅓ cup sugar, 1 teaspoon vanilla, and ½ teaspoon salt.

    Gradually stir rice mixture into egg mixture. Pour into 10x6x2-inch baking dish. Bake, uncovered, at 325° for 30 minutes. Stir; sprinkle with ground cinnamon. Bake till knife inserted halfway between center and edge comes out clean, about 20 minutes more. Serve warm or chilled with cream. Makes 6 servings.

Chocolate Cloud Dessert

    ¾ cup milk
    2 1-ounce squares unsweetened
       chocolate
    ¾ cup sugar
    6 tablespoons butter *or*
       margarine, softened
    1 teaspoon vanilla
    2 eggs
    ¾ cup all-purpose flour
    1½ teaspoons baking powder
    Chocolate Topping

Heat milk and chocolate over low heat, stirring till chocolate melts; cool. Cream sugar and butter; beat in chocolate mixture and vanilla. Add eggs; beat well. Stir flour with baking powder and ⅛ teaspoon salt; blend into creamed mixture. Pour into greased 9x9x2-inch baking pan. Bake at 350° for 25 minutes. Cool; cut. Top with Chocolate Topping. Serves 12.

Chocolate Topping: Whip 1 cup whipping cream till slightly thickened. (Or, prepare 1 envelope whipped topping mix following package directions.) Add 1 cup chocolate ice cream by spoonfuls, beating till mixture mounds. Chill. If needed, beat slightly just before serving.

Gingerbread with Honey Cream

    ½ cup light molasses
    ⅓ cup shortening
    ¼ cup honey
    1 egg
    1½ cups all-purpose flour
    1 teaspoon baking powder
    ½ teaspoon baking soda
    ½ teaspoon ground ginger
    ½ teaspoon ground cinnamon
    Honey Cream

Cream first 4 ingredients. Stir flour with baking powder, soda, spices, and ½ teaspoon salt. Add to creamed mixture alternately with ½ cup boiling water; beat well after each addition. Pour into greased and floured 9x9x2-inch baking pan. Bake at 350° for 20 to 25 minutes. Cut into squares. Serve warm or cool topped with Honey Cream. Makes 9 servings.

Honey Cream: Whip 1 cup whipping cream, 2 tablespoons honey, and ¼ teaspoon ground cinnamon to soft peaks. Makes 2 cups.

Spicy Shortcake

2 cups all-purpose flour
3 tablespoons sugar
1 tablespoon baking powder
½ teaspoon ground cinnamon
¼ teaspoon ground nutmeg
6 tablespoons butter *or* margarine
½ cup chopped nuts
1 beaten egg
⅔ cup milk
1 cup whipping cream
Peach Sauce, Red Berry Sauce,
or Blueberry Sauce

Stir together first 5 ingredients and ½ teaspoon salt. Cut in butter till crumbly; stir in nuts. Mix egg and milk; add to dry mixture. Stir to moisten. Knead gently on floured surface ½ minute. Pat or roll to ½-inch thickness. With floured 2½-inch round cutter, cut into 12 biscuits. Place on ungreased baking sheet. Bake at 450° for 10 to 12 minutes.

Whip cream. Split warm biscuits; fill and top with Peach Sauce, Red Berry Sauce, *or* Blueberry Sauce and whipped cream. Serves 12.

Peach Sauce: Drain one 29-ounce can peach slices; reserve 1 cup syrup. Mix ¼ cup sugar and 2 tablespoons cornstarch; add syrup. Cook and stir till thickened and bubbly; remove from heat. Stir in ½ teaspoon shredded orange peel, ¼ cup orange juice, 2 tablespoons butter *or* margarine, and peaches. Makes 2¾ cups.

Red Berry Sauce: Thaw one 10-ounce package frozen red raspberries; drain, reserving syrup. Add water to reserved syrup to make 1 cup. Halve 2 cups fresh strawberries; set aside. Mix ⅓ cup sugar and 2 tablespoons cornstarch; stir in syrup mixture. Cook and stir till thickened and bubbly; remove from heat. Add ½ *cup* of the strawberries, 2 tablespoons butter *or* margarine, 1 tablespoon lemon juice, and ¼ teaspoon vanilla; stir to mash berries. Cool slightly; gently stir in raspberries and remaining strawberries. Makes 3 cups.

Blueberry Sauce: Combine 1 cup sugar, 2 tablespoons cornstarch, and dash salt; stir in 1 cup water. Cook and stir till thickened and bubbly. Stir in ½ teaspoon shredded lemon peel, 2 tablespoons lemon juice, and 2 tablespoons butter *or* margarine. Stir in 2 cups fresh blueberries. Return to boiling; remove from heat. Cool slightly. Makes 2¾ cups.

Raspberry-Pear Cobbler

Top with dumplings, as shown on page 33 —

1 10-ounce package frozen red
raspberries, thawed
⅓ cup sugar
2 teaspoons cornstarch
¼ teaspoon ground cinnamon
3 medium pears, peeled, cored, and
sliced (2½ cups)
1 cup all-purpose flour
½ cup sugar
1 teaspoon baking powder
1 beaten egg
¾ cup dairy sour cream
2 tablespoons butter, melted

Drain berries; reserve syrup and add water to make 1 cup. In saucepan combine ⅓ cup sugar, cornstarch, and spice; stir in syrup mixture. Cook and stir till thickened and bubbly. Stir in berries and pears; heat through. Pour into 1½-quart round baking dish.

Combine flour, ½ cup sugar, baking powder, and ¼ teaspoon salt. Mix egg, sour cream, and butter; add to flour mixture. Blend well. Drop by spoonfuls atop bubbling fruit mixture. Bake at 350° for 30 minutes. Makes 6 servings.

Cottage Cheesecake Pie

Lemon juice adds tang to this smooth-textured pie —

Graham Cracker Crust
1 12-ounce carton cream-style
cottage cheese (1½ cups)
½ cup sugar
2 eggs
1 tablespoon all-purpose flour
1 tablespoon lemon juice
1 teaspoon vanilla
1 5⅓-ounce can evaporated milk

Prepare Graham Cracker Crust; set aside. Beat undrained cottage cheese till smooth. Add sugar, eggs, flour, lemon juice, and vanilla; mix well. Stir in evaporated milk. Pour into crust. Bake at 325° till knife inserted just off-center comes out clean, 35 to 40 minutes. Chill.

Graham Cracker Crust: Combine 1¼ cups finely crushed graham crackers (about 18 crackers); 6 tablespoons butter *or* margarine, melted; and ¼ cup sugar. Press into 9-inch pie plate. Bake at 375° for 6 to 8 minutes.

Filbert Fancies

1 cup shelled unblanched filberts
1 beaten egg
2 cups sifted powdered sugar
3 tablespoons butter *or*
    margarine, softened
1 teaspoon vanilla
2 1-ounce squares unsweetened
    chocolate, melted and cooled
1 6-ounce package tiny
    marshmallows
1 cup shredded coconut

Coarsely chop filberts; spread on baking sheet. Toast at 350° till golden brown, about 10 minutes. Cool. Combine egg, sugar, butter, vanilla, and dash salt; beat till very light and fluffy. Blend in chocolate. Combine marshmallows and filberts; fold in chocolate mixture. Drop from teaspoon into bowl of coconut; roll evenly to coat. Place on waxed paper-lined baking sheet. Let stand till set. Makes 4 dozen.

Mallow-Nut Fudge

1 10-ounce package tiny
    marshmallows (6 cups)
1 12-ounce package semisweet
    chocolate pieces (2 cups)
2 cups broken walnuts
4½ cups sugar
1 13-ounce can evaporated milk
    (1⅔ cups)
1 cup butter *or* margarine
1 tablespoon vanilla

In bowl combine marshmallows, chocolate pieces, and nuts. In large saucepan blend sugar, evaporated milk, and butter; bring to boiling. Cook and stir over medium heat to soft-ball stage (236°). Remove from heat; stir in vanilla. Pour hot mixture over marshmallow mixture; beat well till chocolate and marshmallows melt. Pour into greased 15½x10½x1-inch baking pan. Cool; cut in 1¼-inch squares. Top with walnut pieces, if desired. Makes 96.

When the candy jar needs refilling, invite family members to the kitchen to share in the joy of candymaking. Those who nurse a "sweet tooth" are sure to find a favorite among *Glazed Cashew Clusters, Jingle Popcorn Balls, Filbert Fancies, Slovakian Nut Candy, Carob Fudge,* and *Mallow-Nut Fudge.*

Carob Fudge

1 cup honey
1 cup peanut butter
1 cup carob powder
1 cup shelled sunflower seeds
½ cup sesame seed, toasted
½ cup flaked coconut
½ cup chopped walnuts
½ cup raisins

In large saucepan heat and stir honey and pea-nut butter just till smooth; remove from heat. Stir in carob powder; mix well. Stir in sunflower seeds and remaining ingredients. Press into buttered 8x8x2-inch baking pan. Chill thoroughly. Cut into 1-inch squares. Store in refrigerator. Makes 2¼ pounds.

Slovakian Nut Candy

1 cup granulated sugar
1 cup finely chopped pecans
1 teaspoon vanilla
⅛ teaspoon salt

In 10-inch skillet heat and stir sugar till melted and golden brown. Stir in pecans, vanilla, and salt. Immediately pour onto buttered board or baking sheet. Roll quickly with buttered rolling pin to 8x8-inch square. Quickly cut candy into diamonds or squares, or break it into small pieces. Makes ½ pound.

Chewy Maple Caramels

1½ cups light cream
1 cup granulated sugar
½ cup packed brown sugar
½ cup light corn syrup
¼ cup butter *or* margarine
1 teaspoon maple flavoring

Line 9x5x3-inch loaf pan with foil; lightly butter bottom and sides. In 2-quart saucepan combine cream, sugars, corn syrup, and butter. Cook and stir over low heat till sugars dissolve. Cook over medium heat to firm-ball stage (248°); stir occasionally. Remove from heat; stir in flavoring. Turn into prepared pan; cool. Turn out on cutting board; cut into 48 pieces. Wrap individually in squares of waxed paper or clear plastic wrap. Makes 48.

Glazed Cashew Clusters

2 cups sugar
1 cup water
¼ teaspoon cream of tartar
2 cups toasted cashew nuts
1 teaspoon vanilla

In 1½-quart saucepan combine sugar, water, and cream of tartar. Cook and stir till sugar dissolves. Bring to boiling; cook to hard-crack stage (300°). Remove from heat; stir in cashews and vanilla. Set pan in larger pan of hot water to keep soft. Drop by tablespoonfuls onto greased baking sheet, forming clusters of 5 or 6 nuts. Makes about 1 pound.

Crunchy Spiced Snacks

1 egg white
½ cup sugar
½ teaspoon ground allspice
½ teaspoon ground cinnamon
2 cups peanuts
1 cup broken pretzels

Beat egg white till soft peaks form; slowly add sugar, allspice, and cinnamon, beating till stiff peaks form. Fold in peanuts and pretzels. Drop from teaspoon in clusters onto greased baking sheet. Bake at 325° till lightly browned, about 20 minutes. Makes 4 dozen.

Jingle Popcorn Balls

12 cups popped corn
2 cups snipped gumdrops
1 cup snipped pitted dates
1 cup light corn syrup
½ cup honey
1½ teaspoons vinegar
¾ teaspoon salt
1 tablespoon butter *or* margarine
1½ teaspoons vanilla

In large bowl combine popped corn, gumdrops, and dates. In heavy saucepan combine corn syrup, honey, vinegar, and salt; bring to boiling. Cook over medium heat to hard-ball stage (260°). Remove from heat; add butter and vanilla, stirring till butter melts. Pour over popcorn mixture, stirring to coat evenly. Form into 2-inch balls. Makes about 30.

Dishes to Tote

Home-cooked food tastes great wherever it is served, but always be sure to keep hot foods hot and cold foods chilled. Many cook-at-home dishes adapt well to travel when prepared with toting in mind. This section offers a selection of make-ahead casseroles, salads, and desserts that are easy to carry and easy to serve. Just remember, foods will stay hot or cold enroute if packed separately in insulated containers.

Spaghetti Bake

Use the lower measure of mozzarella cheese for a more economical main dish casserole —

    1½ pounds ground beef
      1 cup chopped onion
      1 clove garlic, minced
      1 28-ounce can tomatoes, cut up
      1 15-ounce can tomato sauce
      1 4-ounce can mushroom stems and
        pieces, drained
      2 teaspoons sugar
    1½ teaspoons dried oregano,
        crushed
      1 teaspoon salt
      1 teaspoon dried basil, crushed
      8 ounces spaghetti, broken,
        cooked, and drained
      1 to 2 cups shredded mozzarella
        cheese (4 to 8 ounces)
    ⅓ cup grated Parmesan cheese

In Dutch oven cook ground beef, chopped onion, and minced garlic till beef is browned and onion is tender; drain off excess fat. Stir in undrained tomatoes, tomato sauce, mushroom stems and pieces, sugar, crushed oregano, salt, and crushed basil. Bring meat mixture to boiling; boil gently, uncovered, for 20 to 25 minutes, stirring sauce occasionally.

Remove meat sauce from heat; stir in drained spaghetti. Place *half* of the spaghetti-meat sauce in 13x9x2-inch baking dish; sprinkle with shredded mozzarella cheese. Top with remaining spaghetti-meat sauce; sprinkle with grated Parmesan cheese. Bake casserole at 375° for 30 minutes. Makes 12 servings.

Peppy Lasagna

A popular choice for potluck dinners —

      1 pound bulk Italian sausage
    ½ cup chopped onion
    ½ cup chopped celery
    ½ cup chopped carrot
      1 16-ounce can tomatoes, cut up
      1 6-ounce can tomato paste
      1 teaspoon salt
    ½ teaspoon dried oregano, crushed
    ¼ teaspoon pepper
              • • •
    10 ounces lasagna noodles
      3 cups ricotta *or* cream-style
        cottage cheese
    ½ cup grated Parmesan cheese
      2 beaten eggs
      2 tablespoons snipped parsley
    ¼ teaspoon pepper
    16 ounces mozzarella cheese,
        thinly sliced

In skillet cook Italian sausage, onion, celery, and carrot till meat is lightly browned. Drain off excess fat. Stir in undrained tomatoes, tomato paste, salt, oregano, and ¼ teaspoon pepper. Simmer meat mixture, uncovered, for 30 minutes, stirring occasionally.

Cook lasagna noodles according to package directions; drain well. Combine ricotta, Parmesan, eggs, parsley, and ¼ teaspoon pepper.

Place *half* of the noodles in greased 13x9x2-inch baking dish. Spread with *half* of the cheese filling; top with *half* of the mozzarella, then *half* of the meat sauce. Repeat layers. Bake, uncovered, at 375° for 30 minutes. Let stand 10 to 15 minutes. To serve, cut into squares. Makes 10 to 12 servings.

For away-from-home eating, use easy-to-carry containers to pack favorite homemade foods, such as multilayered *Banana Split Cake,* nutty *Raisin Pie* (see recipes, page 63), and *Spaghetti Bake.* These totable foods are great to carry for a tailgate lunch, summer picnic, or church supper.

Ham and Potato Casserole

8 medium potatoes, peeled and
   cubed (8 cups)
3 cups cubed fully cooked ham
¼ cup finely chopped onion
2 tablespoons snipped parsley
1 11-ounce can condensed
   Cheddar cheese soup
1 10½-ounce can condensed
   cream of celery soup
¾ cup milk
1 9-ounce package frozen cut
   green beans, thawed
1 cup soft bread crumbs
   (1½ slices bread)
2 tablespoons butter *or*
   margarine, melted

In greased 13x9x2-inch baking dish layer *half* of the potatoes and *half* of the ham; sprinkle with onion and parsley. Top with remaining potatoes and ham. Mix soups, milk, and ¼ teaspoon pepper; pour over casserole. Cover; bake at 350° for 1 hour. Stir in beans. Toss crumbs with butter; sprinkle atop casserole. Bake, uncovered, 35 minutes more. Serves 12.

Marinated Relish Salad

1 16-ounce can bean sprouts,
   rinsed and drained
2 cups sliced fresh mushrooms
2 cups sliced raw cauliflower
1 medium cucumber, peeled
   and sliced
1 medium green pepper,
   cut in strips
⅓ cup sliced green onion
1⅓ cups vinegar
½ cup sugar
⅓ cup salad oil
1 clove garlic, minced
½ teaspoon salt
12 cherry tomatoes, halved

Combine bean sprouts, mushrooms, cauliflower, cucumber, green pepper, and onion. In large screw-top jar combine vinegar, sugar, oil, garlic, and salt; shake well. Pour over vegetables; toss lightly. Cover; chill several hours or overnight. Before serving, add tomatoes; toss lightly. Makes 12 to 14 servings.

Three-Bean Sausage Bake

1 cup dry navy beans (8 ounces)
1 cup dry red beans (8 ounces)
¾ cup dry garbanzo beans
   (6 ounces)
1 16-ounce can tomatoes, cut up
1 8-ounce can tomato sauce
1 medium onion, chopped
1 teaspoon sugar
8 ounces chorizo *or* smoked
   bratwurst, thinly sliced

Rinse beans separately; drain. In large saucepan combine navy and red beans with 6 cups water. In another large saucepan combine garbanzos and 10 cups water. Bring both pans to boiling; reduce heat. Simmer 2 minutes; remove from heat. Cover; let stand 1 hour. (Or, add beans to water. Cover; soak overnight.)

Add ½ teaspoon salt to garbanzos. Cover; simmer 30 minutes. Drain navy and red beans; add to garbanzos with 1 teaspoon salt. Cover; simmer till tender, about 1 hour. Drain, reserving ½ cup of the cooking liquid.

In 3-quart bean pot or casserole mix reserved liquid, undrained tomatoes, tomato sauce, onion, sugar, and ¼ teaspoon pepper. Stir in beans and sausage. Bake, covered, at 300° for 2 hours. Uncover; bake 2½ hours longer, stirring occasionally. Makes 10 servings.

Potluck Potato Salad

3 tablespoons vinegar
2 teaspoons mustard seed
1½ teaspoons celery seed
3 pounds potatoes, cooked,
   peeled, and cubed (7 to 8 cups)
1 cup chopped celery
½ cup finely chopped green onion
3 hard-cooked eggs, chopped
2 cups mayonnaise *or* salad
   dressing
1 teaspoon salt

Combine vinegar, mustard seed, and celery seed; let stand several hours. In large bowl sprinkle potatoes with a little salt. Add celery, onion, and eggs; toss lightly. Combine mayonnaise, vinegar mixture, and 1 teaspoon salt. Add to potato mixture; toss to mix. Chill thoroughly in 2 bowls. Serves 12 to 15.

Carrot Cake

2 cups all-purpose flour
2 cups granulated sugar
1 teaspoon baking powder
1 teaspoon baking soda
1 teaspoon salt
1 teaspoon ground cinnamon
3 cups finely shredded carrot
    (9 carrots)
1 cup cooking oil
4 eggs

• • •

1 3-ounce package cream cheese,
    softened
¼ cup butter *or* margarine,
    softened
2 cups sifted powdered sugar
1 teaspoon vanilla
¼ cup chopped nuts

In large mixing bowl stir flour with granulated sugar, baking powder, soda, salt, and cinnamon; add carrot, oil, and eggs. Mix till moistened; beat at medium speed of electric mixer for 2 minutes. Pour into greased and floured 13x9x2-inch baking pan. Bake at 325° for 50 to 60 minutes. Cool thoroughly.

Beat cream cheese and butter till fluffy. Slowly beat in powdered sugar till smooth; stir in vanilla. Spread over cake; sprinkle with nuts.

Raisin Pie

Trim with pastry cutouts as pictured on page 61—

2 cups raisins
½ cup sugar
2 tablespoons all-purpose flour
½ cup chopped walnuts
1 teaspoon grated lemon peel
3 tablespoons lemon juice
    Pastry for 2-crust 9-inch pie

In saucepan combine raisins and 1½ cups water; cook, covered, till raisins are plumped, about 10 minutes. Mix sugar and flour; stir into raisins. Cook and stir over low heat till thickened and bubbly. Cook 1 minute more; remove from heat. Stir in nuts, lemon peel, and juice. Line 9-inch pie plate with pastry; turn in filling. Make grape leaf cutouts in top crust; place over filling. Seal and flute edges. Trim with leaf cutouts. Bake at 375° for 40 minutes.

Banana Split Cake

This three-flavored cake is shown on page 61—

1½ cups granulated sugar
1 cup butter *or* margarine,
    softened
4 eggs
½ cup mashed banana (1 large)
½ cup dairy sour cream
½ cup milk
1 teaspoon vanilla
3 cups all-purpose flour
2 teaspoons baking powder
1 teaspoon salt
¼ teaspoon baking soda
¼ cup strawberry preserves,
    cut up
    Few drops red food coloring
½ cup sweetened cocoa mix

• • •

¾ cup sifted powdered sugar
1 teaspoon light corn syrup
¼ teaspoon vanilla
    Milk

In mixing bowl cream together granulated sugar and butter or margarine till light and fluffy. Add eggs one at a time, beating well after each. In small bowl combine mashed banana, dairy sour cream, ½ cup milk, and 1 teaspoon vanilla. Stir together flour, baking powder, salt, and baking soda; add to creamed mixture alternately with banana mixture, beating well after each addition.

Into *1 cup* of the cake batter, fold strawberry preserves and few drops red food coloring, stirring gently *just* till mixed. Into another *1 cup* of the cake batter, fold in cocoa mix; stir gently *just* till mixed.

Spoon *half* of the remaining plain batter into well-greased and floured 10-inch fluted tube pan. Spoon strawberry batter over; carefully spread batter to edges of pan. Cover with remaining plain batter. Spoon cocoa batter on top in a ring; do not spread to edges.

Bake cake at 350° till done, about 70 minutes. Cool for 10 minutes in pan; remove from pan to wire rack. Cool cake thoroughly.

Meanwhile, in bowl combine sifted powdered sugar, light corn syrup, and ¼ teaspoon vanilla. Blend in enough milk (about 1 tablespoon) to make frosting of drizzling consistency. Drizzle frosting over cooled cake.

Menus for All Seasons

Today, just as in the past, social activities often are planned around the serving of a meal. This chapter offers a variety of seasonal menus plus recipes and serving hints designed to trigger your imagination for planning home-cooked meals for any occasion.

On the next few pages you'll find menus for a weekend brunch, a toboggan supper, a hayride cookout, and a fish fry, plus menus for a couple of traditional family events—a holiday dinner and a reunion picnic. And for large group gatherings, there are menus for a block party and a backyard wedding reception.

Since some of yesterday's events are taking on added importance today, menus for a box supper and an ice cream social also are included.

For many generations, families have joined together at the dinner table to celebrate special holidays. The festive meal pictured here includes *Stuffed Turkey, Berry Star Salad, Cottage-Fruit Mold,* and *Cheesed Broccoli.* (See Index for page numbers.)

Cold-Weather Menus

TOBOGGANING SUPPER

Chili Dog Soup
Celery and Carrot Sticks
Sourdough Rye Buns
Chocolate-Nut Bars
Coffee   Milk

Serving Tip: Finish off a fun-filled day of tobogganing by serving a hearty meal to your friends. Offer hungry guests a spicy soup supper set up buffet style so that each person can help himself to the food. Accent the cozy setting by adorning the buffet table with an arrangement of colorful dried flowers and wild grasses.

Chili Dog Soup

- 1 pound ground beef
- 1 pound frankfurters (8 to 10), cut in 1-inch diagonal slices
- 1 28-ounce can tomatoes, cut up
- 2 16-ounce cans dark red kidney beans, undrained
- 2 15-ounce cans tomato sauce
- 1 tablespoon chili powder
- 1 teaspoon salt
- 1 teaspoon dry mustard
- 1 large bay leaf
- 1 cup shredded American cheese (4 ounces)
- ½ cup chopped onion
- Corn chips

In Dutch oven brown the ground beef; drain off excess fat. Stir in frankfurters, undrained tomatoes, undrained kidney beans, tomato sauce, chili powder, salt, dry mustard, and bay leaf; simmer, covered, 30 minutes, stirring occasionally. Remove bay leaf. Serve in bowls; top each serving with a little cheese, chopped onion, and corn chips. Makes 12 servings.

Chocolate-Nut Bars

- ¾ cup butter *or* margarine, softened
- ½ cup granulated sugar
- ½ teaspoon salt
- 2 cups all-purpose flour
- 3 eggs
- 1 teaspoon vanilla
- 1 cup packed brown sugar
- 3 tablespoons all-purpose flour
- ½ teaspoon salt
- 1 6-ounce package semisweet chocolate pieces (1 cup)
- ½ cup chopped nuts
- 1 1-ounce square unsweetened chocolate
- 1 tablespoon butter *or* margarine
- 1¼ cups sifted powdered sugar
- 1 teaspoon vanilla
- Boiling water

Cream ¾ cup butter, granulated sugar, and ½ teaspoon salt. Stir in 2 cups flour. Pat into bottom of 13x9x2-inch baking pan. Bake at 350° till lightly browned, about 20 minutes.

Beat eggs slightly; add 1 teaspoon vanilla. Gradually add brown sugar, beating just till blended. Add 3 tablespoons flour and ½ teaspoon salt. Stir in chocolate pieces and chopped nuts; spread over baked layer. Bake at 350° till golden brown, 20 to 25 minutes.

In saucepan melt unsweetened chocolate and 1 tablespoon butter over low heat, stirring constantly. Remove from heat; stir in powdered sugar and 1 teaspoon vanilla till crumbly. Add enough boiling water (about 2 tablespoons) to make of drizzling consistency. Drizzle over warm cookies. Cool; cut. Makes 3 dozen.

Cheese, corn chips, and onion are popular toppers for *Chili Dog Soup*. Make the soup early in the day, then reheat while winter enthusiasts shed their wraps. Serve with *Sourdough Rye Buns* (see recipe, page 51) and *Chocolate-Nut Bars* for a make-ahead meal that eliminates last-minute fuss.

HOLIDAY DINNER

Stuffed Turkey
Whipped Potatoes   Sweet Potatoes
Buttered Peas or Cheesed Broccoli
Creamed Onions
Berry Star Salad   Cottage-Fruit Mold
Relish Tray
Parker House Rolls   Butter
Honey-Pumpkin Pie or Eggnog Pie
Applesauce-Fruitcake Ring
Coffee   Milk

Serving Tip: While Dad's carving the turkey, pass vegetables, salads, relishes, and rolls to seated family members. To avoid a crowded table, use a sideboard to hold serving bowls. When all have indulged to their limit, clear the table and set up a dessert buffet for each to enjoy at his leisure.

Stuffed Turkey

Serve with the menu shown on pages 64 and 65 —

    1½ cups finely chopped carrot
    ½ cup finely chopped onion
    ½ cup finely chopped celery
    ¼ cup butter *or* margarine
    8 cups dry bread cubes
    ⅓ cup snipped parsley
    2½ teaspoons rubbed sage
    1½ teaspoons salt
      Dash pepper
    1¼ to 1½ cups milk
    1 8- to 10-pound turkey
      Cooking oil

Cook carrot, onion, and celery in butter; mix with bread cubes, parsley, sage, salt, and pepper. Toss with enough milk to moisten.

Rinse bird; pat dry. Salt neck and body cavities; stuff. Tuck legs under band of skin or tie to tail. Place on rack in shallow roasting pan; rub skin with oil. Insert meat thermometer in center of inside thigh muscle, making sure bulb does not touch bone. Cap bird with foil. Roast at 325° till thermometer registers 185°, 4 to 4½ hours.

Berry Star Salad

Frozen raspberries and jellied cranberry sauce complement each other in this festive mold —

    1 3-ounce package raspberry-
      flavored gelatin
    1 3-ounce package lemon-
      flavored gelatin
    1½ cups boiling water
    1 10-ounce package frozen
      red raspberries
    1 16-ounce can jellied
      cranberry sauce
    1 7-ounce bottle lemon-lime
      carbonated beverage
      Crisp greens
      Poached Apple Wedges

Dissolve gelatins in boiling water. Stir in frozen raspberries, breaking up large pieces. Break up cranberry sauce with fork; stir into gelatin mixture. Chill till partially set.

Carefully add lemon-lime beverage, stirring gently. Turn into 6-cup star mold. Chill till firm. Unmold on crisp greens. Garnish with Poached Apple Wedges. Makes 8 to 10 servings.

Poached Apple Wedges: Core 1 apple; cut into wedges. In saucepan bring 2 cups water to boiling. Add apple; return to boiling. Simmer till tender, about 5 minutes. Drain; chill.

Cottage-Fruit Mold

A good-tasting make-ahead salad that leaves you free for other tasks when preparing for guests —

    3 cups cream-style cottage
      cheese (24 ounces)
    2 3-ounce packages orange/
      pineapple-flavored gelatin
    1 13¼-ounce can pineapple
      tidbits, drained
    1 11-ounce can mandarin orange
      sections, drained
    2 cups whipping cream
      Endive
      Orange slices

In large bowl stir cottage cheese with dry gelatin; fold in pineapple and mandarin oranges. Whip cream; fold into fruit mixture. Press into 7- or 8-cup mold. Cover; chill several hours or overnight. Unmold; garnish with endive and orange slices. Makes 12 servings.

Cheesed Broccoli

A quick and simple sauce dresses this vegetable —

2 10-ounce packages frozen
broccoli spears *or* 2 pounds
fresh broccoli
½ cup mayonnaise *or* salad
dressing
¼ cup shredded sharp American
cheese (1 ounce)
1 tablespoon milk

Cook broccoli in small amount of boiling salted water till tender; drain. Combine mayonnaise, cheese, and milk; stir over low heat till cheese melts. Serve over broccoli. Serves 6 to 8.

Eggnog Pie

1½ cups finely crushed
chocolate wafers
6 tablespoons butter *or*
margarine, melted
2 tablespoons sugar
1 envelope unflavored gelatin
¼ teaspoon salt
1 cup milk
3 beaten egg yolks
3 tablespoons rum *or* brandy
3 egg whites
¼ cup sugar
½ cup whipping cream
¼ teaspoon ground nutmeg
Brazil Nut Poinsettias

Mix chocolate crumbs and butter. Press firmly into 9-inch pie plate; chill. Mix 2 tablespoons sugar, gelatin, and salt; stir in milk and yolks. Cook and stir over low heat till mixture thickens slightly and coats a metal spoon. Remove from heat; stir in rum. Chill till partially set. Beat whites till soft peaks form; gradually add ¼ cup sugar, beating till stiff peaks form. Whip cream; fold with whites into custard. Chill till mixture mounds. Turn into crumb crust. Sprinkle with nutmeg; chill till firm. Top with Brazil Nut Poinsettias.

Brazil Nut Poinsettias: Cover unshelled Brazil nuts with cold water. Simmer 3 minutes; drain. Soak in cold water 1 minute; drain. Shell. Cover nuts with cold water. Simmer 3 minutes; drain. Slice lengthwise with vegetable peeler. Place around candied cherries.

Honey-Pumpkin Pie

1 16-ounce can pumpkin
¾ cup honey
1 teaspoon ground cinnamon
½ teaspoon salt
½ teaspoon ground ginger
¼ teaspoon ground nutmeg
¼ teaspoon ground cloves
3 beaten eggs
1 cup milk
1 5⅓-ounce can evaporated
milk (⅔ cup)
1 unbaked 9-inch pastry shell

Combine pumpkin, honey, cinnamon, salt, ginger, nutmeg, and cloves; blend in eggs. Stir in milks. Pour into unbaked pastry shell. (Have edges crimped high to hold filling.) Bake at 375° till knife inserted just off-center comes out clean, about 55 minutes. Cool.

Applesauce-Fruitcake Ring

1½ cups all-purpose flour
1 cup granulated sugar
1 tablespoon unsweetened
cocoa powder
1 teaspoon baking soda
½ teaspoon salt
½ teaspoon ground cinnamon
½ teaspoon ground nutmeg
½ teaspoon ground allspice
1 8½-ounce can applesauce (1 cup)
1 cup chopped pecans
1 cup chopped mixed candied
fruits and peels
½ cup raisins
½ cup buttermilk *or* sour milk
6 tablespoons butter *or*
margarine, melted
Powdered sugar
Whipped cream

In mixing bowl stir together flour, granulated sugar, cocoa powder, soda, salt, and spices. Mix applesauce, nuts, candied fruit, raisins, buttermilk, and butter; pour over dry ingredients. Mix lightly but thoroughly.

Turn into greased and floured 6½-cup ring mold. Bake at 325° for 50 to 55 minutes. Cool 10 minutes in pan; remove from pan. Dust with powdered sugar. Serve with whipped cream.

BOX SUPPER

Super Subs
Dilly Macaroni Salad
Cherry Tomatoes   Sweet Pickles
Banana-Chocolate Cupcakes
Soft Drinks

Serving Tip: To attract the highest bidder, you not only need a tempting "picnic for two" hidden in the box, but also an eye-catching "box." Easy-to-decorate containers include cardboard boxes, canisters, and baskets. When packing the lunch, don't forget to add a colorful cloth and plates to set the picnic mood for you and your new meal mate.

Dilly Macaroni Salad

    1 cup elbow macaroni
    ½ cup sliced celery
    ½ cup chopped green pepper
    ½ cup shredded carrot
    3 tablespoons chopped
        canned pimiento
    3 tablespoons snipped parsley
    ½ cup mayonnaise *or* salad
        dressing
    1 tablespoon vinegar
    ¾ teaspoon salt
    ½ teaspoon dried dillweed

Cook macaroni following package directions; drain well. Cool. Combine macaroni, celery, green pepper, carrot, pimiento, and parsley.

Blend together mayonnaise, vinegar, salt, and dillweed; add to macaroni mixture. Toss lightly. Cover; chill well. Serve salad on lettuce leaves, if desired. Makes 6 servings.

◀ **Pack box-supper foods individually** before placing them in a decorated box. Use clear plastic wrap to keep *Super Subs* fresh and an insulated container to keep *Dilly Macaroni Salad* chilled. Plastic bags or covered servers are good for toting relishes and desserts such as *Banana-Chocolate Cupcakes.*

Super Subs

    2 individual French rolls
    3 tablespoons butter *or*
        margarine, softened
    1 tablespoon prepared mustard
    2 slices cooked turkey *or* chicken
    2 slices boiled ham
    2 slices salami
    2 slices sharp American
        cheese, halved
    ½ small cucumber, thinly sliced
    ¼ cup sliced pitted ripe olives
    2 tablespoons sliced
        green onion (optional)

Split rolls lengthwise; spread cut surfaces with butter, then with mustard. On bottom half of *each* roll, arrange *1 slice* turkey or chicken, *1 slice* ham, *1 slice* salami, and *2 half-slices* cheese. Top with several slices cucumber, olive, and onion. Anchor tops of rolls with wooden picks, if needed. Wrap in clear plastic wrap; chill till serving time. Makes 2.

Banana-Chocolate Cupcakes

    1½ cups all-purpose flour
    1 cup sugar
    1 teaspoon baking powder
    ½ teaspoon baking soda
    ½ teaspoon salt
    1 cup mashed fully ripe
        banana (2 medium)
    ⅓ cup shortening
    ½ cup buttermilk
    ½ teaspoon vanilla
    1 egg
    ½ cup semisweet chocolate pieces
    3 tablespoons chopped almonds
    2 tablespoons sugar

In large mixing bowl stir together flour, 1 cup sugar, baking powder, soda, and salt. Add banana, shortening, ¼ *cup* of the buttermilk, and vanilla; mix till moistened. Beat at medium speed of electric mixer for 2 minutes. Add remaining ¼ cup buttermilk and egg. Beat 2 minutes more. Stir in chocolate pieces.

Fill paper bake cup-lined muffin pans ⅔ full. Mix almonds and 2 tablespoons sugar; sprinkle about ½ *teaspoon* nut mixture atop *each.* Bake at 375° for 20 to 25 minutes. Makes 16.

WEEKEND BRUNCH

Appetizer Fruit Slush
Scrambled Egg Casserole
Link Sausages
Hashed Brown Potatoes or Buttered Grits
Pan-Fried Apples
Biscuits or Muffins   Jelly
Maple Sweet Rolls with Bacon
Coffee   Milk

Serving Tip: When entertaining friends for brunch, use buffet service to lend a casual atmosphere to the occasion and to keep hostess duties at a minimum. If space permits, centralize all of the food in a single area. Otherwise, use a tea cart or small table for the appetizer and the beverages.

Scrambled Egg Casserole

½ cup chopped green pepper
¼ cup butter *or* margarine
12 beaten eggs
• • •
2 tablespoons butter *or* margarine
2 tablespoons all-purpose flour
½ teaspoon salt
⅛ teaspoon pepper
2 cups milk
1 cup shredded American
    cheese (4 ounces)
¼ cup chopped canned pimiento
1½ cups soft bread crumbs
    (about 2½ slices bread)
2 tablespoons butter *or*
    margarine, melted

In 12-inch skillet cook green pepper in ¼ cup butter till tender. Add eggs; scramble just till set. Set aside. In saucepan melt 2 tablespoons butter; blend in flour, salt, and pepper. Add milk; cook and stir till thickened and bubbly. Add cheese; stir till melted. Remove from heat; fold in eggs and pimiento. Turn into 2-quart casserole. Toss crumbs with 2 tablespoons melted butter; sprinkle atop casserole. Bake at 350° for 20 to 25 minutes. Serves 8.

Appetizer Fruit Slush

Mash 2 medium bananas. Blend in one 13¼-ounce can crushed pineapple, undrained; 1⅓ cups orange juice; ⅓ cup sugar; and ¼ cup lemon juice. Mix well. Gently stir in one 12-ounce bottle lemon-lime carbonated beverage. Turn into two 3-cup freezer trays; freeze firm.

To serve, let stand at room temperature 20 minutes. Break into small pieces; stir till mushy. Spoon into sherbets; garnish with 4 or 5 orange slices, halved. Makes 8 to 10 servings.

Maple Sweet Rolls with Bacon

3¾ to 4½ cups all-purpose flour
1 package active dry yeast
1¼ cups milk
½ cup butter *or* margarine
¼ cup granulated sugar
1 teaspoon salt
1 egg
¾ cup butter *or* margarine, melted
⅔ cup packed brown sugar
¼ teaspoon maple flavoring
½ pound bacon, crisp-cooked,
    drained, and crumbled

In mixing bowl combine *1½ cups* of the flour and yeast. Heat milk with next 3 ingredients just till warm (115-120°), stirring constantly. Add to dry mixture; add egg. Beat at low speed of electric mixer ½ minute, scraping bowl. Beat 3 minutes at high speed. By hand, stir in enough of the remaining flour to make a moderately stiff dough. Knead on floured surface for 8 to 10 minutes. Place in greased bowl, turning once to grease surface. Cover dough and let rise till double (about 1½ hours).

Mix ¾ cup butter, brown sugar, and flavoring; divide between twenty-four 2½-inch muffin pans *or* two 9x1½-inch round baking pans.

Punch dough down; divide in half. Cover; let rest 10 minutes. On floured surface roll *each* half to 12x8-inch rectangle; sprinkle each with *half* of the bacon. Roll up jelly-roll fashion, starting with long side. Cut in 1-inch slices. Place in muffin pans, or place *12* slices in *each* round pan. Cover; let rise till double (25 to 30 minutes). Bake at 350° till lightly browned, 25 to 30 minutes. Cool 2 to 3 minutes in pans; invert onto rack. Makes 24.

HAYRIDE COOKOUT

*Hot Apple Brew
Franks with Kraut Relish
Potluck Bean Bake
Roasted Marshmallows
Peanut Sandwich Cookies
Milk*

Serving Tip: Simmer the apple brew at home; tote it to the cookout site in insulated containers to keep the beverage piping hot. Or, assemble the beverage at home and heat over the fire (allow plenty of time for heating). At mealtime, invite everyone to join in the fun by roasting their own franks. Then, pass marshmallows for toasting.

Peanut Sandwich Cookies

½ cup butter *or* margarine,
    softened
½ cup peanut butter
½ cup granulated sugar
½ cup packed brown sugar
1 egg
½ teaspoon vanilla
1¼ cups all-purpose flour
¾ teaspoon baking soda
¼ teaspoon salt
1 cup crisp rice cereal,
    slightly crushed
Peanut butter

In mixing bowl cream softened butter or margarine, ½ cup peanut butter, granulated sugar, and brown sugar till light and fluffy; beat in egg and vanilla. Thoroughly stir together flour, baking soda, and salt; stir into creamed mixture. Stir in cereal. Shape into 2 rolls, 1½ inches in diameter. Wrap in waxed paper or clear plastic wrap; chill thoroughly.

Cut into ¼-inch slices; place on ungreased baking sheet. Bake at 375° for 8 to 10 minutes. Serve plain or frost *half* of the cookies with a little peanut butter; top with remaining cookies, sandwich-style. Makes 60 plain cookies or 30 sandwich cookies.

Hot Apple Brew

4 quarts apple juice *or* cider
1 46-ounce can apricot nectar
8 inches stick cinnamon
2½ teaspoons whole cloves
2½ teaspoons whole allspice
¼ teaspoon ground nutmeg
¼ cup packed brown sugar
1 orange, sliced

In kettle combine juice and nectar. Tie spices in cheesecloth bag; add to kettle with sugar and orange. Cover; bring to boiling. Reduce heat; simmer 15 minutes. Makes 22 one-cup servings.

Franks with Kraut Relish

¾ cup Italian salad dressing
½ cup sugar
1 27-ounce can sauerkraut,
    rinsed, drained, and snipped
¾ cup chopped green pepper
½ cup chopped onion
1 2-ounce can sliced pimientos,
    drained and chopped
24 frankfurters
24 frankfurter buns, split and
    spread with prepared mustard

Heat dressing and sugar till sugar dissolves; cool. Combine vegetables; add dressing mixture. Stir to coat; chill. Cook franks over *hot* coals till done. Drain relish; serve with franks in buns. Makes about 4 cups relish.

Potluck Bean Bake

1 medium onion, chopped
1 tablespoon cooking oil
1 16-ounce can cut green beans
1 15-ounce can garbanzo beans
1 8-ounce can butter beans
2 16-ounce cans barbecue beans
¼ cup packed brown sugar
1 tablespoon Worcestershire sauce
1 tablespoon prepared mustard

Cook onion in oil till tender. Drain green, garbanzo, and butter beans; mix with onion and remaining ingredients. Turn into 2-quart casserole. Bake, covered, at 350° for 1¼ hours. Uncover; bake 30 minutes more. Serves 12.

Warm-Weather Get-Togethers

ICE CREAM SOCIAL

Peach-Cherry Ice Cream
Vanilla Ice Cream
Chocolate-Almond Ice Cream
Assorted Pies and Cakes
Iced Tea   Coffee

Serving Tip: To ripen ice cream, cover top of can with several thicknesses of waxed paper or foil, then replace lid for a tight fit. Plug opening in lid. Pack ice and salt (use 4 parts ice to 1 part salt) around can to fill freezer. Cover with heavy cloth or newspapers. Let ice cream ripen 4 hours.

Peach-Cherry Ice Cream

½ cup sugar
1½ teaspoons unflavored gelatin
4 cups light cream
1 beaten egg
2 pounds fully ripe peaches,
    peeled and mashed (3 cups)
¾ cup sugar
1 cup dark sweet cherries,
    pitted and chopped
2 teaspoons vanilla
¼ teaspoon ground mace
Dash salt

In saucepan combine ½ cup sugar and gelatin; stir in *2 cups* of the cream. Stir over low heat till gelatin dissolves. Slowly stir a small amount of the hot mixture into egg; return all to saucepan. Cook and stir till slightly thickened, about 1 minute; remove from heat. Chill thoroughly.

Combine peaches and ¾ cup sugar; add with cherries, vanilla, mace, salt, and remaining 2 cups cream to chilled mixture. Pour into 4-quart ice cream freezer container. Freeze according to freezer manufacturer's directions. Ripen before serving. Makes about 2½ quarts.

Vanilla Ice Cream

¾ cup sugar
1½ teaspoons unflavored gelatin
4 cups light cream
1 beaten egg
1 teaspoon vanilla

In saucepan mix sugar and gelatin; stir in *2 cups* of the cream. Stir over low heat till gelatin dissolves. Slowly stir a small amount of hot mixture into egg; return all to saucepan. Cook and stir till slightly thickened, about 1 minute; chill. Stir in remaining 2 cups cream, vanilla, and dash salt. Pour into ice cream freezer container. Freeze according to freezer manufacturer's directions. Ripen ice cream before serving. Makes 1½ quarts ice cream.

Chocolate-Almond Ice Cream

5 cups milk
1 cup unsweetened cocoa powder
½ cup light corn syrup
5 eggs
2 cups sugar
3 cups whipping cream
1 tablespoon vanilla
1 cup coarsely chopped
    almonds, toasted

Stir *2 cups* of the milk, cocoa, and corn syrup over medium heat till blended; cool. Beat eggs till foamy; slowly beat in sugar. Blend in cocoa mixture. Add cream, remaining 3 cups milk, and vanilla; mix well. Pour into 5-quart ice cream freezer container. Freeze according to freezer manufacturer's directions. Stir in nuts. Ripen before serving. Makes 4½ quarts.

Smooth and creamy *Vanilla Ice Cream, Chocolate-Almond Ice Cream,* and *Peach-Cherry Ice Cream* make this ice cream social a carnival of flavors. Invite ice cream fanciers to scoop their favorite flavor or combination of flavors into a dish. For à la mode fans, offer a selection of pies and cakes.

FAMILY REUNION PICNIC

Southern Fried Chicken
Baked Red Snapper
Macaroni-Cheese Casserole
Marinated Bean Salad   Potato Salad
Fresh Fruit Salad
Buttered French Bread
Orange-Date Cake
Lemonade   Iced Tea

Serving Tip: If space permits, plan on having the next family reunion in your backyard. Use separate tables for the food and for eating. To speed serving, arrange the food so that family members can move along both sides of the table as they fill their plates. Set beverages on a small table a short distance away from the food table.

Macaroni-Cheese Casserole

1 7-ounce package macaroni,
   cooked and drained
   (about 4 cups)
2 cups shredded sharp Cheddar
   cheese (8 ounces)
½ of an 8-ounce package round
   cheese crackers, crushed
   (1½ cups crumbs)
1 10¾-ounce can condensed cream
   of mushroom soup
1 6-ounce can sliced
   mushrooms, drained
¾ cup milk
¼ cup chopped onion
¼ cup chopped green pepper
¼ cup chopped canned pimiento
   Green pepper rings

Combine cooked macaroni, shredded cheese, *1 cup* of the cracker crumbs, mushroom soup, sliced mushrooms, milk, chopped onion, chopped green pepper, and chopped pimiento. Turn mixture into 2-quart casserole; sprinkle with remaining ½ cup cracker crumbs. Bake at 325° till hot, 45 to 50 minutes. Garnish casserole with green pepper rings. Serves 8.

Southern Fried Chicken

6 whole chicken breasts, halved
   lengthwise (about 4½ pounds)
2 cups all-purpose flour
2 cups buttermilk
   Cooking oil

Season chicken pieces with salt and pepper. Coat chicken with some of the flour, then dip in buttermilk; coat again with remaining flour. In deep skillet heat oil, 2 inches deep, to 325°. Cook chicken, a few pieces at a time, in deep hot oil till done, about 10 minutes, turning once. (Maintain temperature of oil at 325°.) Drain well on paper toweling. Chill thoroughly. Makes 12 pieces.

Orange-Date Cake

The orange syrup is absorbed as the cake cools—

2 cups sugar
1 cup butter *or* margarine
4 eggs
1⅓ cups chopped pitted
   dates (8 ounces)
1 cup chopped pecans
4 cups all-purpose flour
1 teaspoon baking soda
¼ teaspoon salt
1½ cups buttermilk
2 tablespoons grated orange peel
   Orange Syrup
   Whipped cream

In large mixing bowl cream sugar and butter till fluffy. Add eggs, one at a time; beat well after each. Combine dates and pecans; coat with ¼ *cup* of the flour. Stir together remaining 3¾ cups flour, soda, and salt; add to creamed mixture alternately with buttermilk, beating smooth after each addition.

Stir in date-nut mixture. Turn into greased and floured 10-inch tube pan. Sprinkle peel over batter. Bake at 325° for 80 to 90 minutes. Prick hot cake with fork; spoon Orange Syrup over. Cool in pan. To serve, remove from pan. Top with whipped cream; garnish with additional grated orange peel, if desired.

Orange Syrup: In saucepan combine 1 cup sugar, 2 teaspoons grated orange peel, ¾ cup orange juice, and 2 tablespoons lemon juice; heat and stir just till sugar is dissolved.

Orange-Date Cake, Baked Red Snapper, Southern Fried Chicken, and Macaroni-Cheese Casserole are popular picnic fare for family get-togethers during the warm days of summer. To complete this outdoor menu, add an assortment of chilled fruit and vegetable salads, bread, and beverages.

Baked Red Snapper

    1 5- to 6-pound dressed red
          snapper, filleted
       Salt
       Pepper
    3 tablespoons lemon juice
    2 tablespoons butter *or* margarine
    1 12-ounce can vegetable juice
          cocktail (1½ cups)
    ½ cup chopped celery
    ½ cup chopped onion
    ¼ cup chopped green pepper
       Lemon wedges

Place fish in greased 15½x10½x1-inch baking pan. Season with a little salt and pepper. Drizzle with 1½ *tablespoons* of the lemon juice. Dot with *1 tablespoon* of the butter or margarine. Bake at 350° for 20 minutes.

Combine vegetable juice, celery, onion, and green pepper; simmer, uncovered, 10 minutes. Remove fish from oven. Dash with more salt and pepper; drizzle with remaining 1½ tablespoons lemon juice. Pour hot sauce over fish; dot with remaining 1 tablespoon butter. Bake at 350° till fish flakes easily with fork, 30 to 40 minutes; baste occasionally with sauce. Garnish with lemon. Makes 8 to 10 servings.

FISH FRY

Skillet Fried Fish
Potato and Onion Bake
Coleslaw   Sliced Tomatoes
Whole Wheat Bread   Butter
Peanut Brownies
Campfire Egg Coffee

Serving Tip: While the lucky fishermen clean the day's catch, assign someone else the task of building the fire. Prepare the potato-onion mixture in a foil pouch and place on the grill as soon as the fire is hot. When the vegetables are tender, move pouch to the side of the grill to keep it warm, and begin frying the fish. Slice the tomatoes and set out the coleslaw when fish appears almost done.

Potato and Onion Bake

    4 large baking potatoes, peeled
    2 medium onions
    ⅓ cup grated Parmesan cheese
      Salt and pepper
    2 tablespoons butter *or* margarine

Slice potatoes and onions onto a 24x18-inch sheet of buttered heavy foil. Sprinkle with cheese, salt, and pepper; mix lightly on foil. Slice 2 tablespoons butter over all. Seal with double fold. Place on grill; cook over *slow* coals till vegetables are tender, 50 to 55 minutes, turning often. Makes 6 servings.

Campfire Egg Coffee

In small bowl combine ⅔ cup ground coffee and 1 beaten egg (reserve shell). Add ½ cup cold water; blend well. Crumble reserved egg shell and stir into coffee mixture. In saucepan bring 8 cups water to boiling; stir in coffee mixture. Heat and stir over high heat till foam disappears, about 4 minutes. Remove from heat; cover. Let stand 7 to 10 minutes. Serve clear coffee off the top, or pour through fine mesh strainer. Makes 8 cups.

Skillet Fried Fish
Using two skillets speeds the preparation—

    6 fresh or frozen pan-dressed trout
      or other fish (about 6 ounces each)
    ⅔ cup yellow cornmeal
    ¼ cup all-purpose flour
    2 teaspoons salt
    1 teaspoon dried parsley flakes
    ½ teaspoon paprika
      • • •
    1 5⅓-ounce can evaporated
      milk (⅔ cup)
      Cooking oil

Thaw fish, if frozen. Thoroughly stir together yellow cornmeal, flour, salt, dried parsley, and paprika. Dip fish in evaporated milk, then coat with seasoned cornmeal mixture.

Heat a small amount of cooking oil in a large skillet over *hot* coals till hot. Cook fish, a few at a time, in hot oil till lightly browned, 4 to 5 minutes on *each* side. Fish is done when it flakes easily with a fork. Add more oil as needed. Drain fish on paper toweling before serving. Makes 6 servings.

Peanut Brownies

    ¼ cup butter *or* margarine
    2 1-ounce squares unsweetened
      chocolate
    1 cup sugar
    ⅓ cup peanut butter
    2 eggs
    ½ cup all-purpose flour
    ½ teaspoon baking powder
    ½ teaspoon salt
    ½ teaspoon vanilla
    ¼ cup chopped peanuts

In medium saucepan melt butter or margarine and unsweetened chocolate over low heat, stirring constantly. Remove from heat and cool. Blend in sugar and peanut butter. Beat in eggs, one at a time, beating well after each. Thoroughly stir together flour, baking powder, and salt. Add dry mixture to chocolate mixture along with vanilla; beat till batter is smooth. Stir in chopped peanuts.

Pour batter into greased 9x9x2-inch baking pan. Bake at 350° till done, 20 to 25 minutes. Cool on rack; cut into bars. Makes 24.

BLOCK PARTY BARBECUE

Roast Pig   Baked Beans
Cheddar-Macaroni Salad
Sandwich Buns   Butter
Mustard   Catsup
Assorted Relishes
Watermelon
Beer   Soft Drinks   Coffee

Serving Tip: To keep food lines moving at the pig roast, ask more than one person to help carve the meat. Likewise, designate workers to help serve the beans and macaroni salad as people pass by with their plates. To avoid confusion at dessert time, let those in charge of slicing the watermelons work at a table away from the barbecue line.

Cheddar-Macaroni Salad

6 cups medium shell macaroni (21 ounces)
2 cups dairy sour cream
2 cups mayonnaise *or* salad dressing
½ cup milk
1 cup sweet pickle relish
3 tablespoons vinegar
1 tablespoon prepared mustard
1½ teaspoons salt
4 cups cubed Cheddar cheese (16 ounces)
2 cups chopped celery
1 cup chopped green pepper
½ cup chopped onion

In 2 large kettles cook macaroni in a large amount of boiling salted water till tender; drain. Cool to room temperature. Combine sour cream, mayonnaise, and milk; stir in pickle relish, vinegar, mustard, and salt. Toss together cooled macaroni, cheese, celery, green pepper, and onion. Pour dressing mixture over all; toss lightly to mix. (Salad will appear quite moist.) For thorough chilling, refrigerate salad in 2 or 3 large bowls for several hours or overnight. Makes 25 servings.

Roast Pig

Plan on 60 to 70 servings from a pig that weighs about 60 pounds, dressed. (The live weight of the pig would be 90 to 100 pounds.) Choose a grassless place for roasting. In a pit 12 inches deep and as wide and long as the pig, arrange charcoal the length of the pig in 2 rows, 12 to 15 inches apart. Drive notched pipes into ground to hold spit about 16 inches above the coals. Rig up a motor-driven rotisserie or provide manpower to turn the pig throughout the roasting period.

Run spit through center cavity of dressed pig; balance and secure well with wires and/or wire mesh. Tie legs together; cover tail and ears with foil. Have large drip pan under pig, between rows of hot coals. Tilt the pan slightly to collect the fat during roasting.

Place unstuffed pig on spit; begin roasting and turning. As the pig roasts, it will shrink—have tools handy to tighten wires. Also have a sprinkler filled with water to put out any flare-ups among coals. (Fires are more frequent during first or second hour of roasting.) Do not baste pig during roasting.

If coals are added to maintain a constant red glow, a 60-pound pig will be done in about 8 hours. Time will vary, depending upon heat and size of pig. The best indicator of doneness is a meat thermometer. Place thermometer in center of "ham" portion; make sure bulb does not touch bone or spit rod. When thermometer registers 170° to 185°, the pig is done. Have a large, clean surface available for carving. Generally, the meat will be so thoroughly cooked that it will fall off the bones.

Roaster Baked Beans

Preheat electric roaster to 300°*. Empty eight 31-ounce cans pork and beans in tomato sauce into inset pan of roaster; stir in two 14-ounce bottles catsup, 1¼ cups packed brown sugar, 1 cup chopped onion, and 2 tablespoons dry mustard. Sprinkle 1 pound bacon, cut in pieces, over bean mixture. Cook, covered, at 300° for 2 hours. Uncover; cook 2 hours more, stirring occasionally. Makes 25 servings.

*Or, use inset pan in oven. Bake beans, uncovered, at 350° for 3½ to 4 hours; stir often.

WEDDING RECEPTION

Wedding Cake
Pastel Mints   Mixed Nuts
Cinnamon-Fruit Punch   Wine Punch
Coffee

Serving Tip: Center the cake on the reception table, with the punch at one end and the coffee at the other end. Ask guests to form separate lines as they approach, depending on whether they prefer a hot or cold beverage. And don't forget, the top layer of the cake is reserved for the new couple.

Cinnamon-Fruit Punch

Prepare ice ring; freeze. Heat and stir ¾ cup red cinnamon candies with ¾ cup water till candies dissolve; remove from heat. Mix with 6 cups water and five 6-ounce cans frozen pineapple juice concentrate, thawed. Cover; chill. To serve, place ice ring in punch bowl; add juice mixture. Slowly add three 28-ounce bottles lemon-lime carbonated beverage, chilled; mix gently. Makes 42 four-ounce servings.

Wine Punch

Bring 1½ cups water and 1 cup sugar to boiling; boil 5 minutes. Remove from heat. Stir in two 6-ounce cans frozen lemonade concentrate till thawed; chill. To serve, pour lemon mixture in punch bowl. Add three 4/5-quart chilled bottles red Burgundy. Slowly add three 28-ounce bottles ginger ale, chilled; mix. Float lemon slices atop. Makes 46 four-ounce servings.

◀ **Honor the happy bride and groom** with a garden reception after the wedding ceremony. A simple, home-baked *Wedding Cake* topped with pink baby roses adds a special touch to the day's festivities, as does sparkling *Cinnamon-Fruit Punch*. If desired, add a wine punch and coffee to the setting.

Wedding Cake

Repeat basic recipe to create the cake layers —

> 1½ cups granulated sugar
> ¾ cup shortening (12 tablespoons)
> 1½ teaspoons vanilla
> 2 cups all-purpose flour
> 3 teaspoons baking powder
> 1 cup milk
> 5 stiffly beaten egg whites
> Decorator's Frosting
> Flaked coconut
> Red food coloring

For bottom and middle layers: Cream first 3 ingredients. Stir flour with baking powder and 1 teaspoon salt. Add to creamed mixture alternately with milk; beat after each addition. Fold in whites. Bake in greased and floured 13x9x2-inch baking pan at 350° about 30 minutes. Cool 10 minutes in pan; remove. Cool. Prepare recipe 2 more times; bake and cool as above.

For top layer: Halve above recipe, *except* use 3 egg whites. Spread in greased and floured 9x5x3-inch loaf pan. Bake and cool as above. Cover all cakes; let stand overnight to firm.

Prepare 2 recipes Decorator's Frosting. Thin *4 cups* of the frosting with 2 tablespoons water; thinly frost all layers to set crumbs.

Place two 13x9-inch cakes with long sides together on serving tray; frost seam. Mark position for middle layer atop center of bottom layer. Sprinkle marked area with coconut; top with remaining 13x9-inch cake. Likewise, mark position for top layer; sprinkle with coconut. Top with 9x5-inch cake. Dry 1 hour.

Tint ½ *cup* of the remaining frosting pink; cover. Set aside *3½ cups* white frosting; cover. With remaining frosting, repeat frosting cake; smooth with wet knife. Using reserved white frosting and No. 30 decorator tube, pipe rosettes around base of each layer. With same tube, pipe shells atop edge of each layer. Using pink frosting and No. 5 tube, place dot between alternate shells. Let dry. Before serving, top with fresh flowers. Serves 45.

Decorator's Frosting: In large mixing bowl blend 1 cup shortening, 1½ teaspoons cream of tartar, 1½ teaspoons vanilla, and dash salt. Beat in 3 pounds sifted powdered sugar alternately with ¾ cup water; beat till smooth. Blend in 1 teaspoon water at a time, if necessary, to thin to spreading consistency.

Garden Favorites

Ever since the days of the early settlers, home gardens have been a practical means of providing food for the family as well as a source of pride for the gardener. Fortunately, many of the recipes for preserving the bountiful harvest have been passed on from one generation to the next.

This section offers a collection of recipes for relishes, pickles, jams, and jellies. You will recognize some of them as variations of long-standing favorites from your family's recipe file. Others will be delicious new additions to your recipe collection.

Regardless of whether you are a novice at preserving foods or an accomplished canner, you'll enjoy preparing these recipes because of the easy-to-follow directions.

The flavor of homemade relishes is as popular today as ever. Shown here are *Creamy Horseradish Sauce, Frozen Spiced Crab Apples, Best Tomato Catsup, Mango Chutney, Papaya Chutney, Sauerkraut,* and *Dill Pickled Onions.* (See Index for page numbers.)

Time-Worthy Pickles and Relishes

Enjoy garden-fresh vegetables and fruits throughout the year by turning them into tantalizing pickles and relishes. To take the guesswork out of home pickling, follow the easy step-by-step directions given below:

1. Use standard canning jars and lids. Check for flaws; discard any with chips or cracks.

2. Wash and rinse jars. Cover with boiling water; let stand in hot water till needed. Prepare lids following manufacturer's directions.

3. Place water-bath canner containing a rack on heat; add 4 to 5 inches of water. Cover; heat. In another pan heat additional water to add to canner after jars are in place.

4. Pack food into prepared jars following recipe directions, leaving ½-inch headspace.

5. Add hot pickling liquid, leaving ½-inch headspace. Remove air bubbles with knife.

6. Wipe rim of jars with clean, damp cloth.

7. Put prepared lids on jars as follows:

Metal lid with screw band: Place lid, compound side down, on rim of jar. Add band; screw down firmly. Do not loosen band.

Zinc cap with rubber ring: Slip a wet, flexible rubber ring over mouth of jar; fit it against shoulder of jar. Screw cap down firmly against rubber, then unscrew about ¼ inch.

8. Place jars on rack in canner; do not let jars touch. Add additional boiling water to canner till water is at least 1 inch over jars.

9. Count processing time as follows:

Whole cucumbers—fermented or fresh-pack dill pickles: Start timing as soon as you place jars in actively boiling water. Do not wait till water returns to boiling.

Pickles, relishes, and fruit pickles: Start timing when water returns to boiling.

10. Processing times in recipes are for canning at sea level. Add 1 minute to processing time for each 1,000 feet above sea level.

11. After processing, remove jars to draft-free area to cool. Tighten zinc caps, if used.

12. After cooling, check seals. Turn zinc-capped jars upside down; if there is leakage, reseal and process again. For screw-banded jars, look for indentation in center of lids. Wipe jars; label. Store in cool, dark place.

Pepper Relish

Use all green or all red peppers for a change—

    6 sweet green peppers (2 pounds)
    6 sweet red peppers (2 pounds)
    6 medium onions
    1 cup sugar
    1 cup vinegar
    1½ teaspoons salt
    1½ teaspoons dillseed

Wash peppers; remove tops. Finely grind peppers and onions; drain. In large saucepan combine peppers and onions; cover with boiling water. Let stand 5 minutes; drain. To pepper mixture add sugar, vinegar, salt, dillseed, and ½ cup water. Boil gently, uncovered, 5 minutes. Pack into hot half-pint jars, leaving ½-inch headspace. Adjust lids. Process in boiling water bath 5 minutes. (Start timing when water returns to boiling.) Makes 10 half-pints.

Hot Pickled Peppers

Make with banana, paprika, or other hot peppers—

    8 cups red, green, *or* yellow
        peppers (1 pound)
    4 heads fresh dill *or* 2 table-
        spoons dillseed (optional)
    1 cup white vinegar
    2 tablespoons pickling salt
    1 tablespoon sugar
    2 cloves garlic, minced
    ¼ teaspoon crushed dried red
        pepper

Wash peppers; drain. Make 2 small slits in each pepper. (Wear rubber gloves to prevent burning hands.) Pack peppers into hot pint jars, leaving ½-inch headspace. Place *1 head* of the fresh dill or *1½ teaspoons* of the dillseed in *each* jar, if desired. In saucepan combine vinegar, pickling salt, sugar, garlic, red pepper, and 3 cups water; bring to boiling. Pour hot pickling liquid over peppers, leaving ½-inch headspace. Adjust lids. Process in boiling water bath 10 minutes. (Start timing when water returns to boiling.) Makes 4 pints.

Herbs and spices add a distinctive flavor to home-canned pickles, relishes, and jellies. This colorful stack-up includes *Pepper Relish, Basil Jelly, Sweet Pickle Slices, Garlic Okra Pickles, Brandied Peaches, Rosemary Jelly, Hot Pickled Peppers,* and *Sweet Pickled Cabbage.* (See Index for page numbers.)

Garlic Okra Pickles

For crisp pickles, select fresh whole okra pods that are 3 to 4 inches long—

> **3 pounds fresh whole okra pods**
> **1 cup white vinegar**
> **¼ cup pickling salt**
> **2 cloves garlic, crushed**

Thoroughly wash okra; drain. Pack into hot pint jars, leaving ½-inch headspace. In saucepan combine vinegar, pickling salt, garlic, and 3 cups water; bring to boiling. Pour hot liquid over okra in jars, leaving ½-inch headspace. Adjust lids. Process in boiling water bath 5 minutes. (Start timing when water returns to boiling.) Makes 4 pints.

Dill Pickled Onions

Small onions, often called boilers, are used for these tasty pickles (shown on page 82)—

Slice 1½ pounds small onions (1 quart) into ¼-inch slices and separate into rings. Pack in hot pint jars. To *each* jar add 1 head fresh dill *or* 1 tablespoon dillseed and ¼ teaspoon crushed dried red pepper.

In a saucepan combine 2 cups white vinegar, 2 cups water, and 5 teaspoons pickling salt; bring to boiling. Pour over onions in jars, leaving ½-inch headspace. Adjust lids.

Process jars of pickled onions in boiling water bath 5 minutes. (Start timing when water returns to boiling.) Makes 3 pints.

Sweet Pickle Slices

These brine-soaked pickles are shown on page 85 —

> 4 to 5 pounds cucumbers, 3 to 4
>   inches long
> ½ cup pickling salt
> 6 cups sugar
> 4 cups vinegar
> ½ cup prepared horseradish
> 8 inches stick cinnamon
> ¾ teaspoon celery seed

Wash cucumbers. Stir pickling salt into 4 cups boiling water; pour over cucumbers in bowl. Cool. Cover with weighted plate or lid to keep cucumbers in brine. Let stand 7 days.

Drain. Cover cucumbers with hot water; let stand 24 hours. Drain. Cover again with hot water; let stand 24 hours. Drain; slice cucumbers. Mix sugar, vinegar, horseradish, cinnamon, and celery seed; bring to boiling. Slowly pour over cucumbers. Cool; cover. Let stand overnight. Each morning for 4 days, drain syrup from cucumbers. Reheat; pour over cucumbers. Cool; cover. On the fifth day, remove cinnamon; bring cucumbers in syrup to boiling. Pack into hot pint jars, leaving ½-inch headspace. Adjust lids. Process in boiling water bath 5 minutes. (Start timing when water returns to boiling.) Makes 5 or 6 pints.

Sweet Pickled Cabbage

This relish is pictured on page 85 —

> 16 cups coarsely chopped cabbage
>   (about 3½ pounds)
> 2 cups coarsely chopped onion
>   (about 4 medium onions)
> ½ cup pickling salt
> 4 cups sugar
> 3 cups vinegar
> 1 tablespoon mixed pickling spices

Mix cabbage and onion; add pickling salt. Let stand overnight. Rinse; drain. In large saucepan mix sugar, vinegar, and 1½ cups water. Tie spices in cheesecloth bag; add to saucepan with vegetables. Bring to boiling; boil gently, uncovered, 5 minutes. Remove spices. Pack in hot pint or quart jars, leaving ½-inch headspace. Adjust lids. Process in boiling water bath 5 minutes. (Start timing when water returns to boiling.) Makes 6 pints or 3 quarts.

Best Tomato Catsup

Smooth and spicy sauce shown on page 82 —

> 1 cup white vinegar
> 1½ teaspoons whole cloves
> 1½ inches stick cinnamon, broken
> 1 teaspoon celery seed
> 8 pounds tomatoes
> 1 medium onion, chopped
> ¼ teaspoon cayenne
> 1 cup sugar

In small covered saucepan bring first 4 ingredients to boil; remove from heat. Wash tomatoes, peel, remove stem ends and cores, and quarter; drain in colander. In 8- to 10-quart kettle mix tomatoes, onion, and cayenne; bring to boiling. Cook till tomatoes are soft, about 15 minutes; stir occasionally. Put through food mill or coarse sieve; press to extract juice. Add sugar to juice; return to kettle. Bring to boiling; simmer briskly, uncovered, till reduced by half, 1½ to 2 hours. (Measure depth with ruler.) Strain spice mixture into tomato sauce; discard spices. Add 4 teaspoons salt. Simmer till of desired consistency, about 30 minutes; stir often. Pour into hot pint jars, leaving ½-inch headspace. Adjust lids. Process in boiling water bath 5 minutes. (Start timing when water returns to boiling.) Makes 2 pints.

Sauerkraut

Home-cured cabbage, as shown on page 82 —

Use 5 pounds fully matured cabbage; wash, quarter, core, and finely shred. Sprinkle with 3 tablespoons salt; mix thoroughly. Let stand till slightly wilted, 30 to 60 minutes.

Firmly pack cabbage into room temperature jars, leaving 2-inch headspace. Fill with cold water, leaving ½-inch headspace. Adjust lids; screw bands tight. Place jars on pan to catch brine that overflows during curing. Keep cabbage covered with brine. If necessary, open jars and add more brine made by dissolving 1½ tablespoons salt in 4 cups water. Cabbage is cured in 6 to 8 weeks. To process, clean jar rims. Replace lids if sealing compound appears damaged; screw bands tight. Set in water-bath canner filled with cold water; water should cover jars by 2 inches. Slowly bring to boiling. Process 30 minutes. Makes 7 pints.

Corn Relish

Fresh-tasting relish pictured on page 21 —

16 to 20 ears fresh corn
4 cups chopped celery
2 cups chopped sweet red pepper
2 cups chopped green pepper
1 cup chopped onion
2 cups sugar
2 cups vinegar
2 teaspoons celery seed
¼ cup all-purpose flour
2 tablespoons dry mustard
1 teaspoon turmeric

Husk and silk corn. Cook in boiling water 5 minutes; plunge into cold water. Drain. Cut corn from cobs; do not scrape cobs. Measure 8 cups cut corn. In large kettle combine celery and next 3 ingredients. Stir in sugar, vinegar, celery seed, 2 cups water, and 2 tablespoons salt. Bring to boiling; boil, uncovered, 5 minutes, stirring occasionally. Blend ½ cup cold water into mixture of flour, mustard, and turmeric. Stir with corn into hot mixture; return to boiling. Cook and stir 5 minutes.

Pack loosely into hot pint jars, leaving ½-inch headspace. Adjust lids. Process in boiling water bath 15 minutes. (Start timing when water returns to boiling.) Makes 7 pints.

Chowchow

A sweet-and-sour relish shown on page 18 —

Remove stem ends from 5 green tomatoes. Using coarse blade of food grinder, grind tomatoes, 6 green peppers, and 3 large onions. Combine ground vegetables, 2 cups green beans cut in ½-inch pieces, 2 cups cauliflower broken into small buds, and 2 cups fresh corn kernels. Sprinkle with ¼ cup pickling salt; let stand overnight. Rinse vegetable mixture and drain; place in large saucepan or Dutch oven.

Combine 3 cups sugar, 2 cups vinegar, 1 cup water, 1 tablespoon mustard seed, 1½ teaspoons celery seed, and ¾ teaspoon turmeric; pour over vegetables. Bring mixture to boiling; boil gently, uncovered, 5 minutes. Pack hot relish into hot pint jars, leaving ½-inch headspace. Adjust lids. Process in boiling water bath 15 minutes. (Start timing when water returns to boiling.) Makes about 6 pints.

Papaya Chutney

Golden condiment pictured on page 82 —

3 medium papayas, peeled, seeded, and chopped (4 cups)
1 8¼-ounce can crushed pineapple, undrained
1 cup chopped onion
1 cup vinegar
¾ cup packed brown sugar
½ cup light raisins
½ teaspoon ground ginger

In large saucepan or Dutch oven combine all ingredients with ½ cup water and ½ teaspoon salt. Bring to boiling. Reduce heat; boil gently, uncovered, till mixture is of desired consistency, about 30 minutes. Stir occasionally. Pack hot mixture into hot pint jars, leaving ½-inch headspace. Adjust lids. Process in boiling water bath 5 minutes. (Start timing when water returns to boiling.) Makes 2 pints.

Mango Chutney

This accompaniment is shown on page 82 —

1 cup vinegar
1 medium green pepper, chopped
1 small lemon, very thinly sliced and quartered
¾ cup sugar
½ cup chopped onion
¼ cup raisins
1 clove garlic, minced
¾ teaspoon ground cinnamon
¼ teaspoon salt
¼ teaspoon ground cloves
¼ teaspoon ground allspice
⅛ teaspoon cayenne
3 pounds ripe mangoes, peeled and sliced (6 cups)
2 large apples, peeled, cored, and sliced (2 cups)

In Dutch oven combine first 12 ingredients; bring to boiling. Reduce heat; simmer, uncovered, 15 minutes, stirring often. Add mangoes and apples. Simmer, uncovered, till fruit is tender, about 15 minutes; stir occasionally. Pack into hot pint jars, leaving ½-inch headspace. Adjust lids. Process in boiling water bath 5 minutes. (Start timing when water returns to boiling.) Makes 3 pints.

Spicy Pickled Onion Rings, Pickled Eggs, and *Dilled Carrot Sticks* make bold and peppy additions to appetizer trays. Or, serve them as sweet and spicy accompaniments at mealtime. These relishes develop their characteristic flavors as they marinate for several hours in special pickling mixtures.

Plum-Pear Relish

Serve as an accompaniment to roast pork or turkey—

>   2 pounds Italian plums
>   (32 medium plums)
>   1 pound pears (3 medium pears)
>   3 cups sugar

Wash and pit Italian plums. Wash and core pears. Put plums and pears together through food grinder, using coarse blade; measure 5 cups of the fruit mixture. In 8- to 10-quart kettle or Dutch oven stir together fruit mixture and sugar; bring to full rolling boil. Boil hard, uncovered, till syrup sheets off metal spoon, 12 to 15 minutes; stir frequently. Remove from heat and quickly skim off foam with metal spoon. Pour relish at once into hot sterilized jars. Seal with lids. Makes 5 half-pints.

Spicy Pickled Onion Rings

Use beets in a salad or serve as a vegetable—

>   1 16-ounce can beets
>   1½ cups white vinegar
>   ¼ cup sugar
>   6 inches stick cinnamon, broken
>   2 teaspoons whole cloves
>   ½ teaspoon salt
>   1 pound large red onions, sliced
>   and separated into rings
>   (about 4 cups)

Drain beets; reserve juice. Add enough water to juice to make 1½ cups. Add vinegar, sugar, spices, and salt. Simmer, covered, 10 minutes. Strain; pour hot mixture over onions. Chill 4 to 6 hours; stir occasionally. Store in refrigerator. Drain before serving. Makes 4 cups.

Pickled Eggs

1 cup tarragon vinegar
1 cup water
2 tablespoons sugar
1 teaspoon salt
½ teaspoon celery seed
1 clove garlic, minced
2 bay leaves
12 hard-cooked eggs, shelled

In saucepan combine vinegar, water, sugar, salt, celery seed, garlic, and bay leaves. Bring to boiling; simmer, covered, 30 minutes. Cool. Pour over eggs in crock, jar, or bowl. Cover; refrigerate for 2 to 3 days. Drain; serve whole or halved. Makes 12 pickled eggs.

Dilled Carrot Sticks

6 medium carrots (about 1 pound)
1 cup vinegar
¾ cup sugar
1 tablespoon mustard seed
1 head fresh dill *or* ½ teaspoon
    dried dillweed

Peel carrots; cut in 3-inch lengths. In covered saucepan cook carrots in boiling water 10 minutes. Drain; quarter. Combine vinegar, sugar, mustard seed, dill, and 1 cup water; simmer 10 minutes. Add carrots; simmer 1 minute more. Cool. Cover and chill 8 hours or overnight. Store carrots in refrigerator. Drain before serving. Makes 3 cups.

Creamy Horseradish Sauce

This special sauce is pictured on page 82 —

1 6-ounce horseradish root,
    peeled and coarsely chopped
    (1 cup)
⅓ cup light cream
¼ cup vinegar
1 tablespoon packed brown sugar
2 teaspoons prepared mustard
1 teaspoon salt
⅛ teaspoon pepper

In blender container combine all ingredients. Cover; blend thoroughly. In saucepan heat mixture; do not boil. Turn into jar; cover, chill. Store in refrigerator. Makes about 1 cup.

Brandied Peaches

This whole fruit relish is shown on page 85 —

2 cups sugar
2 cups water
2 inches stick cinnamon
6 to 8 small peaches,
    peeled (2 pounds)
Brandy

In medium saucepan combine sugar, water, and stick cinnamon; bring mixture to boiling. Boil hard, uncovered, for 5 minutes. Add a few whole peaches at a time to boiling syrup and cook till peaches can be easily pierced with a fork, 5 to 10 minutes. Remove fruit from syrup; pack cooked peaches in hot sterilized jars. Continue till all peaches have been cooked.

Boil remaining syrup, uncovered, till thickened or until syrup registers 222° on candy thermometer. Remove from heat and cool to room temperature; discard stick cinnamon. Measure syrup; add ⅓ cup brandy for *each 1 cup* of the syrup. Stir well. Fill jars with brandy syrup mixture; seal at once. Store peaches in refrigerator. Makes 2 quarts or 4 pints.

Frozen Spiced Crab Apples

Cinnamon-flavored apples shown on page 82 —

16 small ripe crab apples
1 cup sugar
1 cup water
½ cup red cinnamon candies
3 pieces lemon peel, cut in
    1½x¼-inch strips
6 whole cloves
¼ teaspoon ground ginger
Dash salt

Remove blossom end of crab apples; do not remove stem or peel. In saucepan combine sugar, water, red cinnamon candies, lemon peel, whole cloves, ground ginger, and salt; bring to boiling. Prick apples in several places and place, stem up, in boiling mixture. Return to boiling; reduce heat. Cover; cook over low heat 10 minutes. Do not stir. Remove from heat; cool apples completely in syrup.

Pick apples up by stems; pack in moisture-vaporproof containers. Strain syrup over apples. Seal, label, and freeze. Thaw 1 to 2 hours before serving. Makes 16 spiced apples.

Jams and Jellies for Everyone

Homemade jams and jellies make breakfast a meal your family won't want to miss. They are relatively simple to make and require a minimum of equipment and ingredients. To aid in jelly-making, follow the directions below:

1. Prepare fruit according to recipe.

2. Use standard half-pint jars or jelly glasses. Sterilize jars by boiling them in water 10 minutes; let stand in hot water till needed. Melt paraffin, if used, in top of double boiler over hot water. Or, prepare metal lids following manufacturer's directions.

3. Cook ingredients in 8- to 10-quart kettle or Dutch oven. (A large kettle is needed to prevent boiling over.) Cooking method depends on whether or not commercial pectin is added.

With added pectin: Follow recipe directions. Powdered and liquid pectin are not interchangeable. Use only the type specified.

Without added pectin: For jelly, cook at full rolling boil till it reaches jellying stage. To determine when the jelly is ready, use either the sheeting-off test or a thermometer. The sheeting-off test involves dipping a metal spoon into the jelly, then lifting the spoon and watching for 2 drops that run together and sheet off the spoon. For thermometer test, cook jelly 8° above the temperature at which water boils in your area. (Cook other fruit spreads at a full boil to desired thickness.)

4. Remove from heat; quickly skim off foam.

5. Pour into hot sterilized jars to within ½ inch of top.

6. Seal with paraffin or metal lids and bands.

With paraffin: Spoon *thin* layer of melted paraffin over spread. Using potholder, rotate jar so that paraffin clings to jar above surface of spread. Prick air bubbles. Let harden; repeat. (Total depth should be about ⅛ inch.)

With metal lids and screw bands: Wipe rims of jars. Place metal lids on jars; tighten screw bands. Using potholder, invert jar a few seconds. Turn right side up; cool on rack.

7. When cooled, check seals. For paraffin seals, be sure there are no breaks in paraffin; cover jars. For jars with metal lids, jar is sealed if center of lid remains indented.

Grape Jam

 3½ pounds Concord grapes
 2 cups water
 4½ cups sugar

Wash and stem grapes. (Should have about 10 cups stemmed grapes.) Remove and reserve skins from *half* of the grapes. Leave skins on remaining grapes. In 8- to 10-quart kettle combine the skinless and unskinned grapes. Cover; cook till grapes are very soft, about 10 minutes.

Sieve cooked grape mixture to remove seeds and skins; discard seeds and cooked skins. Measure 3 cups of the strained pulp and return to kettle. Stir in water and reserved uncooked skins. Cook mixture, covered, for 10 minutes. Uncover and stir in sugar. Bring mixture to full rolling boil, stirring frequently. Boil, uncovered, till syrup sheets off metal spoon, about 12 minutes. Remove from heat and quickly skim off foam with metal spoon. Pour jam at once into hot sterilized jars; seal. Makes about 5 half-pints.

Peach Jam

 2½ pounds peaches (8 medium)
 1 1¾-ounce package powdered
   fruit pectin
 2 tablespoons lemon juice
 5½ cups sugar

Peel, pit, and grind or finely chop peaches; measure 4 cups. In 8- to 10-quart kettle or Dutch oven combine peaches, pectin, and lemon juice. Bring mixture to full rolling boil. Stir in sugar. Return to full rolling boil; boil hard, uncovered, for 1 minute, stirring constantly. Remove from heat. Quickly skim off foam with metal spoon. Pour at once into hot sterilized jars; seal. Makes 5 half-pints.

Minted Peach Jam: Tie ½ cup lightly packed fresh mint leaves in cheesecloth bag; press mint with rolling pin to bruise leaves. Add to kettle with peaches, pectin, and lemon juice. Follow directions above for cooking. Remove mint bag and discard before skimming off foam.

Uncooked Strawberry Jam

1 quart strawberries
4 cups sugar
¼ teaspoon ground nutmeg
½ of a 6-ounce bottle liquid
   fruit pectin
2 tablespoons lemon juice

Wash and hull berries; crush thoroughly. Measure 2⅓ to 2½ cups into large bowl. Add sugar and nutmeg; mix well. Let stand 10 minutes. Mix pectin and lemon juice. Add to fruit; stir 3 minutes. Cover loosely; let stand 2 hours. Stir; pour into hot sterilized jars or clean freezer containers. Seal. Let stand till set, 4 to 5 hours. Refrigerate up to 3 weeks or freeze up to 1 year. Makes 5 half-pints.

Gooseberry Jam

2 quarts gooseberries
6 cups sugar
½ of a 6-ounce bottle liquid
   fruit pectin

Wash berries; remove stem and blossom ends. Put through food grinder, using coarse blade; measure 4 cups into large kettle or Dutch oven. Add sugar; mix well. Bring to full rolling boil; boil hard 1 minute, stirring constantly. Remove from heat; stir in pectin. Quickly skim off foam with metal spoon. Pour at once into hot sterilized jars; seal. Makes 7 half-pints.

Tomato Jam

Peel 2½ pounds tomatoes; remove stem ends and cores. In Dutch oven crush tomatoes slightly. Simmer, uncovered, 10 minutes; remove from heat. Measure 3 cups; return to Dutch oven. Add 1 teaspoon grated lemon peel, ¼ cup lemon juice, and ¼ teaspoon salt. Tie 1 tablespoon mixed pickling spices in cheesecloth bag; add to Dutch oven. Stir in one 1¾-ounce package powdered fruit pectin; bring to full rolling boil. Stir in 5 cups sugar; return to full rolling boil. Boil hard 1 minute, stirring constantly. Remove from heat; quickly skim off foam with metal spoon. Let stand 5 minutes. Discard spice bag. Pour at once into hot sterilized jars; seal. Makes 6 half-pints.

Grape Jelly

Concord grapes contain enough natural pectin to make jelly gel without adding commercial pectin —

3½ pounds Concord grapes
½ cup water
3 cups sugar

Wash and stem grapes. (Should have about 10 cups stemmed grapes.) Crush grapes; measure 6½ cups. In large saucepan or Dutch oven combine grapes and the ½ cup water; bring to boiling. Reduce heat; cover and simmer till grapes are very soft, 10 to 15 minutes. Strain cooked grapes and liquid through jelly bag; *do not squeeze.* (Press very gently, if necessary.) Let juice stand overnight in refrigerator.

Strain juice again to remove crystals. Measure juice; add water, if necessary, to make 4 cups. In 10-quart kettle or Dutch oven stir together grape juice and sugar. Bring mixture to full rolling boil. Boil hard, uncovered, till syrup sheets off metal spoon, 8 to 9 minutes. Remove from heat; quickly skim off foam with metal spoon. Pour at once into hot sterilized jars; seal. Makes 4 half-pints.

Basil Jelly

Jars of these brightly colored green and yellow herb jellies are pictured on page 85 —

6½ cups sugar
1 cup white vinegar
6 drops green food coloring
1 cup fresh basil leaves, lightly
   packed
1 6-ounce bottle liquid fruit
   pectin

In large saucepan or Dutch oven combine sugar, vinegar, green food coloring, and 2 cups water. Tie basil leaves in cheesecloth bag; press with rolling pin to bruise. Add to mixture; bring to boiling. Stir in pectin; return to full rolling boil. Boil hard 1 minute; stir constantly. Remove from heat; remove basil bag and discard. Quickly skim off foam with metal spoon. Pour at once into hot sterilized jars; seal. Makes 7 half-pints.

Rosemary Jelly: Prepare Basil Jelly as above, *except* substitute 1 cup rosemary leaves, lightly packed, for basil leaves and substitute 6 drops yellow food coloring for green.

Green Tomato Marmalade

This tomato preserve is shown on page 21 —

3½ pounds green tomatoes
3 cups sugar
½ teaspoon salt
3 lemons
1 cup water

Remove stem ends from tomatoes. Slice tomatoes (about 6 cups). In bowl combine tomatoes, sugar, and salt; set aside. Peel lemons, reserving peel from *one* of the lemons. Remove white membrane from reserved peel; slice peel very thin. In small saucepan combine sliced lemon peel and water. Cover and bring to boiling; boil sliced peel for 8 minutes. Remove from heat and drain, discarding cooking water. Thinly slice lemon pulp and remove seeds.

In large kettle or Dutch oven combine drained lemon peel, sliced lemon pulp, and green tomato mixture. Bring to full rolling boil; boil vigorously till mixture is thickened, about 45 minutes, stirring frequently. Remove from heat; quickly skim off foam with metal spoon. Pour marmalade at once into hot sterilized jars; seal. Makes 4 half-pints.

Golden Lemon Marmalade

1 pound carrots, peeled
2 medium lemons, quartered
    and seeded
3¾ cups sugar
½ cup water
½ teaspoon salt
⅓ cup sliced maraschino cherries

Put carrots and lemons separately through fine blade of food grinder or chop very finely with knife. (Should measure about 3 cups chopped carrot and ¾ cup chopped lemon.)

In large kettle or Dutch oven combine chopped carrot, chopped lemon, sugar, water, and salt. Bring mixture to full rolling boil. Cook over medium high heat for 10 minutes, stirring frequently. Stir in sliced maraschino cherries; cook till mixture thickens and sheets from metal spoon, 3 to 5 minutes longer. Remove from heat; quickly skim off foam with metal spoon. Pour marmalade at once into hot sterilized jars; seal. Makes 4 half-pints.

Pumpkin Butter

1 pumpkin (8 to 9 pounds)
3 cups sugar
2 teaspoons ground cinnamon
½ teaspoon ground nutmeg
½ teaspoon ground cloves

Cut top from pumpkin; scoop out seeds and reserve for drying, if desired. Replace top; place whole pumpkin on baking pan with sides. Bake at 325° till tender, about 3 hours. Leave pumpkin in pan; cut in half to allow liquid inside pumpkin to drain into pan. When pumpkin is cool enough to handle (or completely cooled), scoop out pulp; put through food mill or puree in blender container.

In 4- to 6-quart Dutch oven combine pumpkin purée, ½ cup water, and 2 teaspoons salt. Cook, uncovered, over medium heat till mixture is reduced to 6 cups, 40 to 60 minutes; stir often. Stir in sugar and spices. Bring to full rolling boil; reduce heat. Simmer, uncovered, till thick, 15 to 20 minutes; consistency should be like apple butter. Remove from heat; pour into hot half-pint jars, leaving ½-inch headspace. Adjust lids. Process in boiling water bath 10 minutes. (Start timing when water returns to boiling.) Makes 6 half-pints.

Pineapple-Pear Butter

3 pounds pears (8 medium)
2½ cups sugar
1 8¼-ounce can crushed pineapple,
    undrained
½ cup honey
¼ cup lemon juice

Wash, core, and slice pears; do not peel. In large saucepan combine pears and ½ cup water. Cook, covered, till pears are very soft, about 20 minutes. Remove from heat; put pear mixture through food mill or puree in blender container; measure 3½ cups purée. In 8- to 10-quart kettle or Dutch oven combine pear purée and remaining ingredients; mix well. Boil gently, uncovered, till thick, about 25 minutes; stir often. Remove from heat. Pour into hot half-pint jars, leaving ½-inch headspace. Adjust lids. Process in boiling water bath 10 minutes. (Start timing when water returns to boiling.) Makes 5 half-pints.

INDEX